DAY TRADING

DAY TRADING

*Beat the System & Make Money
in Any Market Environment*

JUSTIN KUEPPER

TYCHO
PRESS

CONTENTS

INTRODUCTION

Depending on whom you ask, the term *day trader* has most people imagining either a wealthy twentysomething trading in front of multiple monitors, or a disheveled gambler losing thousands of dollars in mere minutes.

In reality, a day trader is somewhere in between.

It's true that individuals day trading stocks tend to lose more money than those using a buy-and-hold strategy. In a famous study titled *Trading is Hazardous to Your Health,* UC Berkeley researchers looked at 66,465 households with accounts at a discount brokerage between 1991 and 1996.[1] They found that those trading the most earned 6.5% less than the market average, and only a small subset of them managed to consistently make money from day trading. The researchers attributed the traders' poor performance to overconfidence, which prompted more frequent trading, as well as the tendency to hold on to losing positions and sell winning ones. In some cases, risk-seeking also led traders to under-diversify their portfolios by investing almost all of their money in only one or two stocks.

These tendencies have led many financial experts to compare day trading to gambling. In some ways, the analogy makes sense. Most day traders act like gamblers, their trading informed by emotion, all the while paying commissions to brokers for the privilege. Combine that with data that shows most day traders lose money, and the comparison with gambling becomes inescapable. That's why many experts recommend that the average person stick to long-term investing as the best way to generate passive income from the financial markets.

A better analogy for day trading, however, would be the game of poker.

Like the average poker player, the average day trader does not trade for a living. The average poker player loses money in the long run, just as the average, nonprofessional trader loses money in the long run. Everyone in a poker room must pay a rake to the casino; likewise, everyone in the market must pay commissions to a broker. What makes poker different from other games is that there are gamblers who make a consistent living by playing *better than others* at the table. In a study of 415 million hands of poker, economist and statistician Randall D. Heeb found that the skill of a poker player had "a statistically significant effect on the amount of money won or lost."[2] The same goes for day trading: Some professionals are able to consistently make money, and more often so than others.

Professional day traders employ detailed trading strategies and sound money management techniques to steer clear of the problems most amateurs face—such as overconfidence. Using statistical analysis techniques, professional day traders identify high-probability trades and act on them with precision in order to generate a quick profit, while limiting their overall risk exposure. By contrast, amateur day traders often haphazardly enter a trade, see the stock moving lower, become worried about mounting losses, and prematurely sell the stock before it rises again.

Here's an example: An amateur and professional day trader both identify a promising stock exhibiting a potential breakout chart pattern. The amateur might invest half of his total account value in the stock in the hopes of a breakout, whereas the professional determines the trade's upside and downside potential, and then decides to invest 5% of his account value. The stock subsequently moves 5% lower. The amateur may worry—especially given the large investment—and sell at a loss, whereas the professional knows that the 5% decline is still within their bounds and decides to let the trade continue. The stock then moves 20% higher in a breakout. The amateur didn't have a plan and let fear guide his decisions; the professional, on the other hand, had a well-defined plan and ended up profiting from the trade.

The good news is that professional day trading is a learned skill. It is something that most people can master by devoting enough time, energy, and capital. Similarly, it's possible to learn how to play the odds and become a professional poker player. This book is written for people who are looking to become professionals at day trading, whether it's something they end up doing full-time, or just to supplement their income. In this book you'll learn the mechanics of the markets, common day trading strategies, and tips for finding an edge in one of the most competitive industries in the world.

Many people who claim to be experts at day trading sell guides to novice day traders for a lot of money. In reality, the day trading strategies that work today won't work tomorrow, and there is no single strategy that works for everyone. If there was, day traders could simply retire and let computers place trades on their behalf all day! Like professional poker, day trading is a profession that requires an instinct for reading the market and identifying promising trades. This book is designed to provide you with a solid level of knowledge of day trading and show you how to develop these instincts over time.

We will also prepare you for the emotional roller coaster that day trading is. The SEC itself—the regulatory body governing trading and investing—warns that "most individual investors do not have the wealth, time, or temperament to make money and to sustain the devastating losses that day trading can bring." This book will not only discuss money management strategies to avoid these devastating pitfalls, but also describe techniques for dealing with the stress and emotional volatility that are unique to the day trading profession.

In the end, the goal of this book is to help you decide whether day trading is a good fit for you; provide you with a basic grasp of the methodology and its application; and show you the path to becoming a better day trader.

THE MARKET

Most people are familiar with the "market" in a layperson's sense. When they go to the supermarket to buy groceries, they understand that the store is essentially a place where buyers and sellers meet to exchange goods (e.g., foods). The picture becomes less clear when one turns on the television and sees media pundits discussing "the market's performance." It can be unclear what market they are talking about, or how the stock and bond markets work.

In this section, we'll look at markets from a conceptual standpoint, and give you an overview of the functioning of financial markets such as stocks and futures.

WHAT IS THE MARKET?

Suppose that a grocery store in Florida expects the price of orange juice to rise significantly over the coming month and wants to stock up on its supplies. The grocery store could go to an orchard and request 15,000 pounds of orange juice, but it would be difficult to settle on a fair price and find a seller that would be able to supply the full amount. As a result, the grocery store might have to identify multiple sellers, buy orange juice at different prices, and then try to calculate its future costs. In addition, the grocery store would have to coordinate delivery and incur storage costs for all this orange juice (carrying costs).

The futures market makes buying 15,000 pounds of orange juice trivial. By purchasing a $20,000 futures contract for 15,000 pounds of orange juice to be delivered the following month, the grocery store can conduct business as usual and still know that it will be able to offset any potential higher prices with the profit derived. The grocery store could then turn around and sell the futures contract for a profit on its expiration date, without even taking delivery of the product. In the end, the grocery store's bottom line would be the same as if it had actually accepted delivery.

On the other hand, suppose that a farmer is looking to sell 15,000 pounds of orange juice. Not only would the farmer have to coordinate all of the buyers, he would also have to come up with the cash to grow the oranges before realizing any profit. Again, the futures market makes selling 15,000 pounds of orange juice very simple: The farmer puts the contract up for sale, receives the proceeds from the contract, and then supplies the goods at a future time. The transaction makes the farmer's income more stable, and enables him to receive a fair price.

The futures market, the stock market, and other markets are mediums for facilitating transactions between buyers and sellers. Instead of individuals and companies having to negotiate small private transactions among themselves, financial markets provide greater transparency so that everyone knows they received a fair market price, which was created by matching a given product's supply with its demand. In most cases, these transactions take the form of an auction, to ensure the best possible price for both parties. The electronic nature of modern markets also helps lower transaction costs, and gives anyone with an Internet connection access to trading contracts, assets, securities, and other products worldwide.

What does this mean for day traders?

Using the same orange juice example, suppose that a day trader notices an unusual spike in demand for orange juice futures. The trader could purchase the contract for $20,000, wait the course of the day for the price to rise to $21,000, and then sell the contract for a $1,000 profit (or 5% gain)—all within the same day. In doing so, the trader purchases the rights to 15,000 pounds of orange juice and can sell those rights to a different party for a nice profit.

Day traders help make markets more efficient by including all relevant information in the price of an asset. Drawing on the above example, suppose that a farmer in Brazil was selling the orange juice futures contract without knowing that there was a spike in U.S. demand for oranges due to a drought in Florida. The market ensures that the information about the drought is automatically included in the latest price, since the day traders would have closed the price gap very quickly. As a result, the farmer in Brazil knows that the current price reflects all of the information available to the market, even if he himself does not possess all of that information.

These dynamics highlight just how powerful global markets have become. Day traders, long-term investors, and end users come together to determine fair prices for everything—from commodities like orange juice to companies like Apple. For day traders, there are literally hundreds—if not thousands—of different markets to trade in, and therefore countless opportunities to gain profit. These profits are derived from capitalizing on changing expectations and speculating where market prices are headed based on the information available.

WHERE DOES THE MONEY COME FROM?

The first question that many aspiring day traders ask themselves is, "Where does the money come from?" At first glance, the market seems like a zero-sum game where there are winners and losers. This is true for markets like futures and options, where there is always a winning and a losing side to every transaction. However, other financial markets like the stock market are not necessarily zero-sum games.

A company whose stock is consistently rising can produce many winners and no losers. The stock may never come down to its original levels if the company is able to continue generating revenue and profit growth. Such dynamics make the stock market a powerful tool for wealth creation in society, as economies drive wealth creation at a faster rate than inflation destroys it.

The corollary to this is that there are instances in these same markets when everyone loses. During the 2008 economic crisis, one might wonder where all the money that had been lost by banks and investments had gone. The answer is that the price the market is willing to pay for such assets can simply decrease, and the assets become less valuable—even if nobody makes a single trade; after all, any asset is only worth as much as someone is willing to pay for it. A second great example of this phenomenon has to do with what happens when a company goes bankrupt: The money invested wasn't necessarily "taken" by executives—it simply disappeared, along with the expectations that the investors had had for the company's future.

The good news is that stock prices have trended higher historically due to the economy's positive rate of growth, which, in turn, has made the stock market a powerful tool for wealth creation, at least for those who participate in it.

As mentioned earlier, futures and options are two instances in which the market does function as a zero-sum game. A farmer making $20,000 by selling the rights to 15,000 pounds of oranges that he plans to grow next month will lose out if prices rise to $25,000 by next month, whereas the grocery store that purchased the futures contract will pay $5,000 less than the market price that month. While there are some exceptions, most options contracts operate the same way: Someone selling the rights to their stock at a certain price will lose out if the stock rises above that price before the contract expires.

In the end, market prices are determined by supply and demand. When more people want to buy an asset, the asset's price increases, and vice versa. Rumors, the news, and one's own earnings—among other factors—influence a trader's perception of a company, commodity, or asset. These perceptions in turn influence supply and demand, and, therefore, price changes.

HOW DOES THE MARKET WORK?

Suppose a day trader places a market order of 500 shares of Apple stock after determining that the price is likely to rise in the future. Although the shares appear on his computer screen nearly instantly, there are actually a number of different steps that need to be executed executed in just milliseconds to make this happen. Day traders should familiarize themselves with these steps, so as to ensure that they are getting the best possible prices and to prevent costly mistakes.

Stocks are originally created or issued in the primary market via public offerings, such as an Initial Public Offering (IPO). Once issued, these stocks are traded in the secondary market between traders and investors. This trading process doesn't involve the company at all. Large institutional traders usually dominate initial public offerings and then sell shares to smaller retail traders, although retail traders can also secure some of these shares with the help of their brokers.

Most day traders start their interaction with the market by communicating—either online or by phone—with a *broker* trading in the secondary market. Since trading is a regulated activity, brokers are necessary intermediaries who, in exchange for a fee or commission, buy and sell stocks or other assets on behalf of individuals or institutions. Instead of communicating with their clients personally, most modern brokers have online platforms that execute instant transactions, thus making trading a largely hands-off task that is still highly secure and regulated.

Brokers buy and sell stock on behalf of their clients, either on an *exchange* or over the counter. In general, most trades occur over exchanges like the NYSE, NASDAQ, or NYMEX, although many derivatives trade over the counter in deals made directly between the buyer and seller rather than through an intermediary. Exchanges are responsible for matching buyers and sellers. In the past, specialists handled the process on a trading floor where loud shouting and lots of shoving used to take place, with tons of paper lying around. Most modern exchanges have switched to electronic processes in order to improve efficiency and enforce controls.

Exchanges maintain lists of buyers and sellers in what is known as an *order book.* On one side, there are "bids," which represent prices and amounts that buyers are willing to pay for a security. On the other side, there are "asks," which represent prices and amounts that sellers are willing to accept for their security. Matching engines are used to determine which orders can be fulfilled. When a bid and an ask are matched, a new market is made, and the trade price becomes the security's new price.

The entire process works like this: A day trader places an order of 500 Apple shares with his broker. The broker's system combines this trade with other orders of Apple shares from other client accounts, and submits a big order for the stock to an exchange. The exchange checks the order book and fills the buy order with the best prices available. The exchange then sends the shares to the broker. The broker divides up the shares among its clients, and the number of shares that each day trader ordered appears on his screen, along with the transaction details.

Still, knowing *how* the market works is not enough. You also need to know *who* is involved in all of the processes that take place.

KEY MARKET PLAYERS

Being a powerful tool for wealth creation, the market has attracted some of the world's brightest minds. According to the Wealth-X Billionaire Census, finance represents the single largest source of wealth for the world's billionaires![3] Among these billionaires are corporate executives, market makers, institutions, hedge fund managers, and—finally—individual retail traders. It's important for aspiring day traders to know how all of these individuals and institutions interact before jumping into the ring with them.

Issuers are undoubtedly the most important players in the market. They create the securities that everyone else trades. By selling stock, companies raise money to support their growth and create liquidity for existing investors (including company founders) by enabling them to sell some of their shares. Companies can also influence the market through stock buybacks, dividends, and mergers and acquisitions ("M&As"). In commodities markets, producers fill a similar role by generating oil and other commodities that are sold in the market, and can influence prices by changing the supply.

After issuers and producers supply the raw materials, *market makers* are responsible for keeping the market for these materials moving. Market makers compete for orders by displaying buy and sell quotes for guaranteed shares; by starting out with a block of shares, they profit by simultaneously buying stock at the bid price and selling stock at the ask price. Market makers *must* maintain continuous two-sided quotes within a predefined spread to generate profit. By constantly executing these small trades, they accumulate a profit over time, and ensure that the market is *liquid*—that is, that trades can be easily executed at fair prices for everyone.

For example, suppose that IBM stock is trading with a bid/ask spread of 96.80/96.90. A market maker could simultaneously enter an order to sell IBM stock at 96.90 and an order to buy them at 96.81. If a trader somewhere decides to sell at 96.81, the market maker has *made the spread* by selling their shares at 96.90 (via the existing ask), and buying them back at 96.81. The market maker makes a profit of 0.09 per share, assuming that someone bought the stock at 96.90 before a seller offered it at 96.81. These types of trades ensure that any investor can buy IBM stock whenever he wants, and know what the price will be with a reasonable degree of certainty.

Market makers are incentivized to be involved in as many trades as possible so as to maximize their profits on the basis of the small profit they receive on each trade. They are also contractually obligated to contribute bid and ask orders to the market. Since brokers are looking for the best prices for their clients, market makers with the tightest and fairest quotes tend to generate the most profit. Even though such sentiments are common in many retail day trading circles, market makers *are not* in the business of ripping off their clients—doing so would only jeopardize their relationships with clients.

In the 1950s, individuals owned over 90% of the stock in U.S. corporations, but *institutional investors* have since taken the reins. These days, only 30% of individuals control their own stock. A growing number of people now rely on mutual funds and other investment firms to manage their stocks for them.

The number of mutual funds has grown from just 100 in the early 1950s[4] to more than 10,000.[5] These funds alone have attracted trillions of dollars in investment capital, and this does not even include pension funds and other forms of institutional investment.

Institutional investors include large organizations such as banks, pension funds, or insurance companies that make substantial investments in securities. These investments are often made through financial institutions (including mutual funds and hedge funds), which trade the money on the investors' behalf. Such groups tend to control the majority of the trading volume on most exchanges, although the bulk of that volume comprises long-term investing rather than short-term trading.

However, there are many groups that use active trading strategies, like high frequency trading (HFT) operations. According to a 2010 report by the U.S. Securities & Exchange Commission, HFT operations accounted for more than half of all U.S. equity trading volume in 2009.[6] These groups use sophisticated algorithms to rapidly trade securities and profit from small discrepancies in security prices. The use of HFT has fallen since 2009, but the practice continues to generate a significant amount of trading volume in U.S. equity markets.[7]

Regulators have been working hard to even out the playing field, by limiting the ability of these institutions to unfairly profit off individuals. For instance, some HFT institutional traders have been accused of *front running*: They would see an order for a given stock placed by an individual, move to the front of the line using high-speed data connections, buy the stock at a lower price before the individual gets to it, and then sell that stock to him immediately for a profit. In such a scenario, the individual loses out because he pays a higher price than he would otherwise have had to pay for the stock.

Retail traders, which include day traders, constitute the smallest group in the market. These traders generally work for themselves or in partnership with other traders. They trade using their own capital or other people's money. Although most day traders in the past were institutional traders, the advent of direct-access brokers and powerful communication tools has made it possible for anyone to compete. Day traders who use other people's capital are known as *proprietary traders,* or *prop traders* for short. Prop traders generate profit for themselves by taking a cut of what they make off the capital provided by a hiring firm or individual. Modern regulations have also prevented many financial institutions from having prop-trading desks so as to prevent potential conflicts of interest.

Typical transactions between these parties may look as follows: An entrepreneur comes up with a great idea and decides to start a company using his own money. Eventually he decides that it's time to raise money to fund the company's growth and let someone else take over the reins. The company goes public via an IPO for $1 million. The entrepreneur then sells his shares for cash to the investment bank that sponsored the IPO. The investment bank goes on a roadshow, selling the stock to market makers and other parties for a profit of $1 million, thus making the company worth $2 million. The market maker then creates liquidity for the stock, and retail traders are able to buy and sell easily.

The above example raises the question: How do day traders and other parties know how much to pay for a stock?

PRICES, PATTERNS & TRENDS

Let's say you are shown a stock chart and asked to determine whether or not to buy the company's stock based on changes in its price over time. While it might seem ludicrous to make an investment decision based on nothing but price, prices themselves can actually tell a detailed story about a company. Based on past movement, price statistics are able to predict where prices are most likely headed. Patterns in price fluctuation could also provide insight into the market's underlying psychology.

A rising stock may indicate a successful company that is steadily growing, or it could be indicative of a promising young company on the verge of growing rapidly and generating a large windfall. A falling stock may suggest that a company is facing growth problems or is in danger of going bankrupt. Similarly, a stock that is starting to trend lower for the first time in years may suggest new issues within the business and herald the beginning of the end. A company whose stock is starting to trend higher for the first time may have undergone successful restructuring, and the stock could lead to higher profits in the long run.

The most important element for day traders in any market is the price, which is usually defined at any given moment as the price of the most recent successfully executed transaction between a buyer and seller. A company's fundamentals should not really matter if the market is efficient and if all current information is already included in the stock price. In order to run some statistics and gauge the market's psychological state, the only thing that really matters is where the price is headed, and perhaps how the price has moved in the past.

How do you determine where prices are headed?

On a micro level, future prices are determined by looking at the order book—the existing bid and ask prices. If there are more ask prices than bid prices, it means that there are more sellers than buyers and the price is likely to decrease, and vice versa. Large gaps between bid and ask prices signal potential price volatility to come, as they indicate a higher level of indecision when it comes to what is considered a fair price. High frequency trading (HFT) is a form of day trading that looks at order books to determine where prices are headed in the next two seconds.

On a macro level, prices tend to form patterns and trends based on the underlying psychology of the market and the performance of the asset in question. A company reporting consistent growth will likely see prices trend upward, whereas a commodity seeing less demand will likely see its prices trend downward. Price patterns can also be very telling when it comes to getting a feel for market sentiments. Most retail day traders focus on these elements when trying to determine where prices may be headed over the coming seconds, minutes, or hours.

Trends play a particularly important role in the life of a day trader. Prices of stocks either trend one way or the other, especially within longer timeframes. Trends occur in the market because of *herd behavior*, which occurs when individuals in a group behave without centralized direction; it is a phenomenon that has been studied by scientists, including Nobel laureates like Vernon

Smith, Amos Tversky, Daniel Kahneman, and Robert Shiller. Taking advantage of these trends can enable day traders to increase their chances of placing successful trades.

Finally, day traders prefer liquid markets to illiquid (or less liquid) ones, because the prices in liquid markets are more certain. It would be very difficult to pinpoint a buying price for a stock that has a wide bid/ask spread and has not traded in days, and even more so to sell the stock on the same day. A highly-traded stock like Apple or a popular index exchange-traded fund (ETF) on the other hand, might have a tight bid/ask spread, which is to say that day traders would be able to purchase the stock at a well-defined price, and would be able to count on exiting the position with equal certainty. That said, illiquid assets are and should be priced based on existing orders and demand rather than current market prices, which may be out of date.

QUICK RECAP

- The market consists of buyers and sellers exchanging assets on a centralized exchange. By connecting supply with demand in one spot, prices become fully transparent, liquidity is greatly improved, and regulators are able to put rules in place to protect both parties.

- The supply side of the financial market consists of publicly traded companies, which sell stock in initial public offerings (IPOs) and other offerings; commodity producers, which mine, grow, or otherwise produce raw materials for sale; and other parties that put up assets (or rights to assets) for sale.

- Market makers are responsible for creating liquidity on a day-to-day basis by buying at the bid, selling at the ask, and profiting from the bid/ask spread. Without market makers, it would be difficult for buyers and sellers to connect in financial markets.

- Institutional traders consist of hedge funds, mutual funds, and other parties that buy and sell large quantities of assets for various reasons. Given their large amount of capital, they account for the vast majority of trading volume.

- Retail traders consist of individuals who buy and sell small quantities of assets in order to generate a profit. Although individuals used to constitute the bulk of the market, they have been eclipsed by institutional traders and are now very much the minority.

- There are many types of financial markets, including stock markets, commodities markets, and foreign exchange markets. In addition to trading different assets, traders have access to financial derivatives, such as options and futures.

- Some markets, like options and futures, are zero-sum markets. Other markets, like the stock market, are not zero-sum, since the market can rise consistently over time, generating profits for all. In general, given the upward bias, it is easier and less risky to trade in positive-sum markets than to trade in zero-sum markets.

- Many traders use price patterns and statistics to gauge the market's psychology at a given point in time before determining the optimal times for buying or selling.

- Trends provide the best opportunities for traders to profit, because prices are moving in a predictable direction. Most traders adhere to the saying "The trend is your friend" when trying to profit in the financial markets.

‖‖‖‖‖‖‖‖‖‖‖‖‖‖‖‖‖‖

2

THE TRUTH ABOUT TRADING

The day trading industry, riddled with promises of wild success as well as dire warnings of failure, makes it difficult for beginners to evaluate objectively. As always, the reality lies somewhere in between, and aspiring traders should carefully weigh the benefits and risks involved before jumping headfirst into the market.

In this section, we explore the truth about trading, and discuss what to expect when getting started in the industry.

WHY TRADE?

There are few professions in the world that offer unlimited financial potential, flexible working hours, and constant intellectual stimulation.

With the advent of the Internet and the liberalization of financial markets, anybody can now trade stocks, bonds, futures, currencies, and countless other assets from anywhere in the world. New day traders can start out with little more than a small starting capital, a working Internet connection, and a brokerage account. Experienced day traders can make six-figure incomes just by working relatively few hours every day, and without having to leave the house. The combination of low barriers to entry and high earning potential is what attracts some of the brightest minds in the world to this industry.

A typical day for a retail day trader begins before the market opens. During this time, the day trader screens for potential opportunities by reading the news or looking at statistical indicators. The first half hour after the opening bell is usually the most chaotic. The market typically displays significant volatility during this time, as overnight information is being digested and acted on. A day trader can take advantage of stabilizing trends during the mid-morning, when things start to normalize and before larger institutional traders in New York break for lunch. The second wind begins mid-afternoon, when additional opportunities may present themselves on the basis of new information in the form of news and/or statistical measures. After the market closes, the day trader spends a bit of time catching up on market action, and setting reminders to follow up on particular trades during the next trading session.

U.S. markets usually open at 9:00 a.m. and close at 4:00 p.m. eastern time. As such, day traders put in limited hours of work each day. On the West Coast, day traders have even more attractive work hours, which begin around 6:00 a.m. Pacific time, and end around 1:00 p.m. Pacific time. These attractive work hours leave the day trader with the rest of the afternoon and night for leisure activities.

WHY DAY-TRADE?

Most financial experts recommend purchasing long-term investments instead of trying to time the market by day trading. As mentioned earlier in this book, statistics show that over time, active traders tend to generate lower returns than long-term investors. The reasons for this phenomenon are unclear, but it could be that most people are not willing to commit the time and capital necessary for learning and mastering a challenging profession like day trading.

So why would anyone choose to day trade?

As the market produces an average return of only about 8% each year, long-term investing requires either a lot of capital or a long time horizon to pay off. During the first year, someone with a capital of $25,000 might make $6,250, which is hardly enough to sustain a living. An investor would need about $200,000 in the first year in order to make a $50,000 income—*before tax*. Of course, these relatively low rates of return are justified for investors purchasing broad market index funds, as they usually do not have to lift a finger in order to make a profit. An annual return of 8% also beats most, if not all, savings account interest rates and other forms of saving or investing capital.

In contrast, day traders attempt to generate higher rates of return by devoting more time and resources to trading. With the same $25,000 in initial capital, day traders may identify trades that return an average of 1%. An average position size of $5,000 would mean that each trade could generate an average of $50 in profit, with many different trades placed each and every day. In aggregate, these activities could generate much higher returns than long-term investing could, making them sufficient for earning a part-time or full-time living.

The Good News

Day trading is a profession that's easy to start but difficult to master.

An aspiring day trader needs little more than sufficient starting capital, a brokerage account, and a reliable Internet connection to get started. There are also countless resources online for learning about day trading and coming up with ideas; for example, StockCharts (www.stockcharts.com) provides free stock charts and access to hundreds of technical analysis tools, and StockTwits (www.stocktwits.com) provides real-time stock picks suggested by amateurs and professionals who use the website. These are just two of thousands of online tools that help make day trading easier than ever.

Trading itself has also become increasingly accessible over the years. In the past, day traders had to use already outdated information as they placed orders over the phone. Today, the Internet brings real-time information to our fingertips and makes placing trades as easy as clicking a button. Automated day trading strategies do not even require pressing a button—using a set of rules that the day trader specifies beforehand, a computer algorithm can automatically place trades on his behalf.

Many aspects of day trading are poised to become even easier for retail day traders as new technology levels the playing field. New analytical tools and trading platforms also promise to make it increasingly easy to develop high-performance trading systems, which could eventually rival many institutional-grade ones.

INTERNET-BASED

Day trading has shifted from an institution-only activity to something accessible to anyone with an Internet connection. Over the past several years, the Internet has dramatically reduced the cost of doing business, by eliminating many unnecessary intermediaries from the process. As a result, commissions and related fees have been reduced significantly, and the market has become much more accessible to day traders. For example, before the 1980s, brokerage commissions were fixed at 1% of the trade amount. In 1975, the SEC made fixed commissions illegal, leading to the rise of discount brokerages. The rise of the Internet has put downward pressure on commissions ever since.

The availability of the Internet in nearly every part of the world has made day trading a very location-agnostic profession. Although many day traders would prefer to have very stable and fast Internet connections, they are ultimately free to live nearly anywhere with a connection. Day traders on the extreme end of the spectrum have taken up residence in developing countries, where the cost of living is low and they are thus able to day trade full-time. Others may prefer to work from the comfort of their own home rather than worry about maintaining an office.

By connecting billions of people, the Internet has made information more accessible for everyone. The lightning speed of Internet connectivity means that day traders have access to real-time prices and market-moving information, instead of having to wait to read about developments in the next day's newspaper. Services like The Fly on the Wall (www.theflyonthewall.com) provide real-time news to day traders, who can then take advantage of opportunities as soon as they arise. The information gap between institutional and retail day traders is rapidly closing.

At the same time, the rise of web-based applications that operate entirely on the Internet has dramatically broadened the number of tools available to day traders. From trading system exchanges to stock screening tools, these services provide day traders with an extensive set of instruments at their disposal. The ongoing growth in cyberspace will likely create even more opportunities in the future for day traders.

Finally, the ubiquity of smartphones makes it possible to trade on the go, while having access to the same real-time tools and information. In addition to trading, users can use their smartphones to access a growing number of apps that can assist with trading. For instance, StockTwits provides access to real-time ideas and information from anywhere, and AnalystRT provides real-time alerts when analysts release new market-moving research reports.

BONUSES & INCENTIVES

Each year, day traders execute transactions in the order of hundreds or thousands—substantially more than the average individual investor. As a result, day traders are tremendously profitable for brokers, who usually earn a commission on each one of these trades. Brokers work hard to attract day traders by offering them incentives and bonuses, ranging from free trades to outright cash, simply for moving over their accounts. Taking advantage of these bonuses and incentives enables day traders to reduce their trading costs or earn a little extra on top of their trading income.

Some of the most common types of incentive include:

- Reduced commissions
- Improved execution speed
- Enhanced flexibility
- Higher-end trading platforms

For example, for a new account with $50,000, a typical promotion might be 60 days' worth of free trades and up to $600 in cash. Many brokers also cover any fees incurred when transferring from a prior broker, so as to eliminate any extra costs that transfers may impose on the day trader. Often, day traders can also request unadvertised discounts, and save money in other ways. These unadvertised discounts include reduced commissions over the long term, and can add up to significant savings over the course of months or years.

In addition to financial benefits, day traders have access to a number of other technological benefits, such as improved trading platforms and faster execution speeds, which provide them with an edge over others in the market. These tools make it easier for day traders to identify profitable trading opportunities before long-term investors get the chance to act. Such trading platforms are usually provided to the general market for a monthly fee, but qualified day traders can gain free access to them by meeting monthly trading minimums.

The Bad News

Day trading is one of the hardest professions to master.

With its potential for generating very high returns, financial trading has attracted some of the smartest and most talented people in the world. Harvard sent nearly a third of its graduating class of 2008 to firms where they would work as bankers, traders, or investors. Many of these talented individuals work at institutions where they have significant capital at their disposal, and some have even branched off to form their own hedge funds. Either way, these *competitors* have both deep pockets and a sophisticated knowledge of the markets.

Aside from the competition, retail day traders are also at the bottom of the stack when it comes to the economies of scale associated with trading. Institutional investors have large amounts of capital and place large amounts of trades, so they pay less in commissions, and have access to much more sophisticated analytic tools; retail day traders often end up paying a lot more in commissions and have access to fewer analytical tools, which place them at an immediate disadvantage vis-à-vis competitors in the market.

The high capital requirements of day trading and the tendency to use borrowed money for trading also add more risk to being a retail day trader. Given that a minimum bankroll of $25,000 is needed to day-trade, many retail day traders are putting a substantial portion of their net worth at risk. Trading on margin may increase the profit potential of smaller amounts of capital by enabling traders to borrow enough capital to cover up to half of each trade.

Leverage is a double-edged sword, however, and can also accelerate one's losses if used irresponsibly. After all, by borrowing money you are on the hook for more than the amount of capital that you possess, including interest on the borrowed funds.

In its online posting titled *Day Trading: Your Dollars At Risk*, the SEC itself issues a sobering warning to would-be day traders:

- Be prepared to suffer severe financial losses.
- Day traders do not invest.
- Day trading is an extremely stressful and expensive full-time job.
- Day traders depend heavily on borrowing money or buying stock on margin.
- Don't believe claims of easy profit.
- Watch out for "hot tips" or "expert advice" from newsletters or websites.
- Remember that "educational seminars," classes, and books about day trading may not be objective.
- Check out day trading firms with your state securities regulator.

Day traders must overcome tremendous odds in order to generate a consistent profit in the market, and many people simply are not cut out for the job. It often takes several years for retail day traders to generate any profit, and several more years for them to generate a full-time income—assuming they can afford the early losses and eventually become proficient at the job. The industry is also becoming increasingly competitive, with the rise of high-frequency trading and algorithmic trading, which facilitate capitalizing on opportunities in mere milliseconds.

MINUS-SUM GAME

Day trading is often considered a *minus-sum* game, as retail day traders start out at a disadvantage compared to institutional traders. With the odds stacked against them, retail day traders must overcome these odds by generating higher real profits than institutional traders, while using the same information and contending with a great number of competitors.

A retail day trader may make a $5,000 trade with a $10 commission and incur an immediate loss of 0.2% due to the commission, whereas an institutional trader may make a $50,000 trade with a $5 commission and incur a loss of only 0.01%. As mentioned earlier, institutional traders may also have faster access to information, which could be used to gain a competitive edge that goes beyond economies of scale in executing transactions.

In many ways, the minus-sum game is similar to the way casinos work, in that the house takes a cut and puts all gamblers at an immediate disadvantage. While it is still possible for one to generate consistent winnings and make a full-time living just by beating out other players at the poker table, it is even easier to do so if he starts out with a lot of money and plays at higher-stakes tables. It also takes more effort to earn money than it would if everyone started out on an equal footing and the casino did not take a cut.

COMMISSIONS

Commissions are the single largest expense incurred by many day traders, given the sheer volume of trades they execute. Often, the most important consideration for day traders is the size of the trade rather than the commission amount itself. The same flat-fee commission eats up a bigger chunk of smaller trades than larger trades. For this reason, retail day traders are at an immediate disadvantage compared to institutional day traders. Unfortunately, many day traders underestimate or fail to take into account these effects in their performance reviews.

There are three types of commissions:

- *Flat-fee* Flat-fee commissions are fixed charges for a transaction that do not take into account the number of shares being bought or sold.
- *Percentage-based* Percentage-based commissions are variable charges based on the value of the trade, such as 1% of the trade value capped at $20.00.
- *Combination* Combination commissions are a combination of the flat-fee and percentage-based commissions.

Commissions have trended significantly lower over time—particularly for day traders—as competition among brokers heats up and systems become increasingly automated. Many online brokers are already offering traditional investors commission-free trading, a practice which could eventually spill over to the day trading market where a greater number of transactions take place. These brokers are focused on making money from a combination of interest on cash balances and margin interest on funds, which day traders borrow to leverage their returns.

For some brokers it is important to make sure that trades are being executed at NBBO (National Best Bid and Offer) prices. By receiving compensation from market makers for order flow, and executing trades at less-than-favorable prices, the zero-commission brokers of the 1990s actually cost traders a lot of money. While many of these practices no longer exist, it is still advisable to double-check that low commissions are a good deal with no hidden costs.

Finally, day traders should always try to negotiate lower commissions over time. The "published rates" on many broker websites represent their highest rates, with discounts widely available for those placing a high number of trades. In general, many brokers are willing to negotiate downward by around 20% to 30%, depending on the size of the day trader's account and the number of transactions he executes each year. These relatively small discounts can add up to a lot of money over time, so it pays to negotiate!

There are also a number of different ways for day traders to reduce their commissions over time, depending on the type of commissions they are being charged:

- *Larger Trades* Placing larger trades would mean that a smaller percentage of the overall value is being paid in commissions. A trader being charged $10 to execute a $1,000 trade is paying 1% in commission, but a trader being charged $10 to execute a $10,000 trade is paying only 0.1%, which is a lot less to make up.
- *Fewer Trades* There is no rule about how many trades day traders can or should place in a single day, but those placing a high number of trades are typically paying more in commissions than those placing a lower number of trades. Limiting the number of trades per day can help keep commissions in check.

SLIPPAGE

Most retail day traders do not have immediate access to the trading floor, so their trades are required to move through several intermediaries before being executed. While orders are being routed through third parties, the bid and ask prices of the negotiated security could change. These dynamics are known as *slippage,* and they can have quite an impact on a day trader's bottom line, especially since day traders place many trades and rely on narrow price movements in order to generate profits.

In simple terms, slippage is the difference between the *expected* entry and exit points, and the *actual* price received. Slippage can have a significant effect on a day trader's bottom line, while the actual impact is less predictable than the fixed and predictable costs associated with commissions and exchange fees.

The amount of slippage incurred depends on several factors:

- *Liquidity* The liquidity of a market is the largest predictor of slippage, with illiquid markets experiencing greater variability than liquid markets.
- *Asset Class* Slippage varies depending on the asset class being traded, since different asset classes have different order execution mechanisms.
- *Order Routing* Slippage tends to be greater for orders that are routed through several market makers rather than those placed directly with a single market maker.
- *Order Type* Market orders are subject to slippage because they are executed at the "best price," whereas limit orders have a hard limit on the execution price.

One way to avoid slippage is to use limit and stop orders instead of market orders. However, in such cases, day traders risk missing opportunities. Often they must decide whether the risk of missing a particular trade outweighs the risk of executing the trade at a worse-than-expected price. In the event that big trades go unexecuted, slippage could lead to fewer gains, greater losses, or significant missed opportunity costs.

The most common solution to the slippage problem is to use limit orders when entering a position, and stop orders when exiting a position. By placing these types of orders, day traders ensure that they are getting a specified or better price with each trade. There is still the chance that the trade will not be executed, but the risk is mitigated by ensuring that the limit and stop prices are conservatively placed when it is highly desirable to execute a trade.

Day traders should also be mindful of slippage when they are creating trading systems. It is important to account for slippage when simulating trades based on historical price datasets—a process known as *backtesting*. If day traders fail to account for slippage, the predicted returns for trading systems can differ substantially from the actual returns generated. These dynamics are especially relevant for trading systems that rely on high-volume strategies like scalping to generate a profit, as the slippage on each trade adds up over time to account for larger dollar amounts.

BID/ASK SPREADS

The difference between the bid and ask price for a given security is known as the *bid/ask spread,* which largely depends on the security's *liquidity*—that is, the number of shares bought and sold. In general, securities that are highly liquid have *tighter* bid/ask spreads, and those that are less liquid have *wider* bid/ask spreads. The bid/ask spread can vary with time, even when one is looking at the same security. How it varies is based on a number of factors, including times when the stock is volatile due to earnings or news releases.

Day traders can compare liquidity between securities by calculating the percent spread. To do this, they would divide the difference between the bid and ask prices by the ask price, and then multiply that number by 100. For example: a security with a bid of $3.34 × 200 and an ask of $3.53 × 200 has a bid/ask spread of $0.19 / $3.53 × 100, or approximately 5.4%. This figure is much higher than a blue-chip stock like Apple Inc., which may have a bid/ask spread of well under 1% most of the time. For day traders, a lower bid/ask spread percentage is indicative of a better deal, as they would likely be able to buy and sell without incurring immediate losses.

Day traders primarily focus their efforts on highly liquid assets such as S&P 500 index futures or blue-chip stocks like Apple Inc., for which the bid/ask spread percentage is lower rather than illiquid stocks or other securities. Those who do trade in illiquid securities, or in liquid securities that become illiquid, could end up losing money from the bid/ask spread. For example, a hot stock may normally have a narrow bid/ask spread, but the same stock after earnings could see its bid/ask spread widen significantly. It is important to consider these dynamics if one wants to avoid getting caught in a tough situation.

PROFESSIONAL COMPETITION

Day traders face intense competition in the financial markets. Each day, billions of dollars are traded across numerous stock exchanges by a combination of institutional investors, institutional traders, retail investors, and retail traders. While these various groups are all competing to generate above-market returns, retail day traders have the most demanding requirements of all in terms of required returns. After all, making money in the market is not that difficult—it is *beating* the market that is more challenging.

Professional day traders working for hedge funds or other institutions are better trained, better capitalized, and have access to more information than the majority of retail day traders. These factors give professional day traders in the market an immediate edge over retail traders. By trading with their clients' capital, they do not have the same emotional connection to that money, but are still incentivized to perform. These incentives include the possibility of earning 2% of assets under management, or—in the case of hedge funds—getting bonuses amounting up to 20% of profits made during the year.

For the most part, professional competition comes in two forms: proprietary trading firms and algorithmic trading firms. Proprietary trading firms are institutions that provide capital to professional day traders (or *prop traders*) in exchange for a cut of their profits. Some successful professional day traders begin working at a prop-trading firm using their capital, before eventually transitioning to paying the firm a reduced commission trading their own capital in the market, with a high amount of leverage to improve their profitability.

Algorithmic trading firms, also known as *algo traders*, prefer to use computer programs developed by quantitative traders (or *quants*) to trade on their behalf. Doing so removes all human emotion from the equation, and dramatically improves execution times. High-frequency trading operations use similar computer programs to execute thousands of trades per millisecond, so as to take advantage of any opportunity in sight. In fact, these programs often end up cancelling about 90% of open orders and executing on only 10% of opportunities—which, according to data from the SEC, are the best of the best.[8]

The professional competition in the market is constantly on the rise, as technology becomes cheaper and people become smarter. At the same time, many hedge funds have hired some extremely smart people like physicists and mathematicians in an attempt to find even the slightest edge that they can exploit for profit. With lock-up periods for client funds and greater access to capital resources, professional competitors may also be better equipped than retail traders to weather the market's turbulence.

The emergence of neural networks,[9] genetic algorithms, and other forms of artificial intelligence software could make competing in markets even more difficult in the future. By analyzing millions of real-time transactions, these systems can quickly identify price patterns and trends that would be impossible for any individual to see. The proliferation of these systems on a wider scale in the future could have a tremendous impact on the profitability of retail day traders within the market, as researchers continue to explore different possibilities offered by technology.

Many experts believe that these trends will force retail day traders to either take bigger risks or increasingly rely on luck in order to generate above-market returns.

MANAGING EXPECTATIONS

It is hard to know what to expect when getting started on day trading, with a combination of success stories and dire warnings from financial professionals. Before getting started, it is important for would-be day traders to have the right expectations about how much money they could possibly make, and a good understanding of the risks involved in one of the most competitive industries.

Realistic Goals

Many people think day trading will make them rich overnight. After all, trades that make 5% of $100 and generate $5 in profit could theoretically make 5% on $10,000 dollars, and generate $500 in profits. Becoming rich is simply a matter of borrowing more money on margin in order to commit to day trading, right? Unfortunately, the many holes in that theory make such returns unrealistic for day traders.

For example, suppose that a day trader with an account valued at $100,000 has a 50% chance of making a 5% return. With a $100 trade generating $5 in profit, he is assuming a relatively small amount of risk in the event that the trade does not turn out, since he would lose less than $100 in total. By placing a $10,000 trade in order to make $500, he would also be putting 10% of his entire account at risk, and could lose up to $10,000 in absolute terms. Although the percentages are the same, retail day traders are concerned about absolutes as well, especially when they consider the emotional impact of losing $100 versus $10,000.

When trading as a business, it is important for day traders to set realistic goals and make sure their plans are viable. These goals and expectations are often based on the amount of starting capital a day trader has, and how much risk he is willing to take. Those who start with a large amount of capital willing to take higher risks stand to make greater amounts of money than those who start with low amounts of capital willing to take lower risks. Of course, many retail day traders find themselves on the risk-averse end of that spectrum.

What would be a realistic goal for day traders?

Most professional day traders *target* a 20% to 30% return each year, although novice retail day traders may struggle to reach those levels. While returns should exceed the market's 8% per annum average to justify the effort, novice day traders may only break even in the first year or two as they learn the ropes and refine their strategy. It is also important to realize that 20% of a $25,000 account is only $5,000 per year, which is not an adequate full-time income for most people. In order to generate $50,000 per year at those levels, a day trader would need $250,000 in capital, an amount in capital that is not always feasible for novice day traders to have, or advisable for them to risk.

Just because professional day traders *target* 20% to 30% per year does not mean that they are successful every year. Day trading returns often depend on the right market conditions for success. Volatility—or the range of price movement over a period of time—plays one of the biggest roles in day trading returns. Exceptionally volatile market conditions, like those of the 2008 financial crisis, create many lucrative opportunities for day traders. During quieter, less volatile times, it can be much more difficult to beat the market's returns by trying to buy and sell at opportune times. Retail day traders should be prepared to handle the swings that come with day trading, and weather the droughts when few opportunities present themselves.

The last key point to keep in mind when setting expectations is that the amount of return generated often correlates to the amount of risk taken. For instance, it is certainly *possible* to generate an annual return of 50% rather than 10%, but it would involve taking on significantly greater risk by borrowing money and buying on margin. A better metric to measure performance is *risk-adjusted return*, which accounts for many of these increased risks. As we mentioned earlier in this book, retail day traders are being forced to take on increasing levels of risk in order to generate the kinds of returns they would need to succeed.

During periods of low volatility, day traders may be forced to increase their leverage in order to capitalize on smaller opportunities and maintain their performance. This leverage adds risk to a day trader's portfolio, and could decrease risk-adjusted returns during quiet times.

Most Will Lose

The majority of retail day traders will be unsuccessful in beating the market's average returns according to the results of a number of different studies showing that returns decline in a trading account as the number of trades increase. In addition to overall underperformance, those just getting started in day trading face a steep learning curve that usually equates to losses during the first year or two, while they familiarize themselves with the market. The combination of these factors suggests that those new to the market will almost certainly lose money, at least until they gain enough experience, and the majority will continue to lose money afterwards.

To go back to the poker analogy made at the beginning of the book: The percentage of professional poker players out of all those who play poker is extremely low. People who want to become professionals must deal with not only professional competition, but also with a game that's stacked against them in the first place by the casino's rake. While it is naive to say that there are no professional poker players, the argument could be made that many of them experience uneven wins and losses over time, thus skewing their ability to remain profitable.

Of course, the findings from day-trading studies are skewed based on experience and education, where those with the least experience tend to lose more than those with the most experience. There are many examples of successful day traders in many different markets, and there is no doubt that the human brain is smarter than any current computer algorithm when deciphering complex systems. The key point to realize is that the most successful day traders are usually professionals with extensive education, experience, and resources.

Minimum Bankroll

Securities regulators mandate that *pattern day traders* start with and maintain at least $25,000 in capital at any given time in order to remain in compliance. In addition to the capital requirements, pattern day traders must also trade only in margin accounts. Regulators believe that these requirements will keep amateur day traders from introducing significant default risk into the market by trading in smaller leveraged brokerage accounts.

FINRA rules define a pattern day trader as anyone who executes four or more "day trades" within five business days, provided that the number of day trades represents more than 6% of the trader's total trades in the margin account for that same five-business-day period. In addition to these rules, FINRA provides broker-dealers with the right to designate pattern day traders using their own criteria that may be even stricter than FINRA's rules. Day traders can contact their broker to learn more about their pattern day trader classifications.

If a day trader falls below that level, a minimum equity call will be issued, and the trader will either have to commit new capital to bring the account back up to the $25,000 level or be forced to hold positions for a 90-day period to be reclassified as a non-pattern day trader.

One Big or Many Small

Many day traders and investors talk of their big wins in the market. For example, Warren Buffett began purchasing Coca-Cola stock back in 1988 and has since made over 1,700% in capital gains on the stock, on top of its steadily rising dividend payments. These stories may be impressive for value and growth investors, but day traders are focused on much smaller gains that they accrue over a short period of time instead of large gains over a long period of time.

A day trader might buy $10,000 worth of a stock at the beginning of the day and sell the position for $10,170 at the end of the day, netting a $150.00 profit after paying $20 in commissions and slippage. While $150 may not seem like a lot of money, it is a 1.5% return made in a single day, and would translate to an annualized return of over 70%. These types of returns would significantly surpass Mr. Buffett's ~18% annual returns in his portfolio.

Profit Goals per Trade

Most day traders will not be able to make a consistent 1.5% return every day just from their trading. If they could, they would be more successful than the world's greatest investor. In fact, most day traders will not even be able to stick to a specific percentage or dollar amount profit over a period of time. The problem with these specific targets is that they incentivize traders to take unnecessary risks in order to reach an arbitrary point for the day—after which, instead of continuing to look for opportunities, the traders allow themselves to rest on their laurels.

In reality, many successful day traders abandon these specific profit goals. Instead, they focus on effectively executing their strategy to generate income over the long term. This *process-over-profit* mentality allows traders to focus more on the overall efficacy of their strategy rather than its performance over a single day. Instead of worrying about daily performance, time can be spent backtesting the strategy and honing its performance over time.

Remaining Calm

Day trading is widely considered to be one of the most stressful jobs in the world. Unlike a traditional 9-to-5 job, day traders are risking their entire fortune each day in order to grind out a small profit, and an entire week's worth of gains can be wiped out in just seconds. A large part of the stress involved in trading is attributed to its inherent uncertainty. Also, decisions need to be made in seconds, not minutes or hours. Remaining calm under these stressful conditions can be extremely difficult, even for traders with nerves of steel.

The most successful day traders are characterized by virtues like calmness, patience, and decisiveness. On some days, day traders will have very few trading opportunities and will need to wait on the sidelines. Other days, they will need to choose between many different opportunities and exercise calmness and decisiveness.

The key to successfully acting on these opportunities is to have a plan beforehand. A sudden gap lower after an earnings announcement can be an unexpected setback for a day trader. The novice trader's immediate reaction may be to quickly liquidate the entire position in order to stop the losses, but an experienced trader may instead have a rule in place that requires him to sell half the position and wait for a turnaround before selling the rest. As a result, the experienced trader may catch a rebound to recoup some of his losses.

MYTH-BUSTING

The popularity of day trading as a "get rich quick" scheme in the 1990s has led to a number of myths being perpetuated throughout society.

There's a Secret to Success

Search for the keyword "day trading" on any search engine, and you will find hundreds and thousands of results promising outlandish returns over time "With a small investment of just a few thousand dollars, you will have immediate access to a system that has consistently generated 15% every month since 2003. The best part is that this secret strategy requires just minutes of time each day to place trades, and then you can relax!"

Sadly, there is no guaranteed system that makes 15% every month. If such a system existed, its creators could turn a mere $1-million investment into $4.35 million within a single year. The power of compounding could go on to generate trillions of dollars over a very short period of time, something that obviously has never been done before. As the adage goes, "There is no such thing as a free lunch." In this case, there is no secret magic system.

Day traders must instead put in the work each day in order to find and capitalize on opportunities in the market. The work they have to do includes screening for stocks, analyzing charts, and identifying potential entry and exit points. The only "secret" to success is developing an edge and an instinct for trades over time through diligent research and a lot of practice. These instincts take years to develop.

You Don't Need Much Money

Another common misconception in the market is that very little capital is needed to make a lot of money from day trading. These myths are perpetuated in part by brokers offering tremendous amounts of leverage in non-securities markets.

In the futures and forex markets, day traders can start with as little as $50 or $100, and attempt to generate a profit using a leverage of 500-to-1 or greater. These dynamics make it seem like a large profit can be made with a small amount of money. After all, a $100 account leveraged 500-to-1 may purchase $50,000 worth of a currency that might move 2% over a period of time. The 2% gain on $50,000 would generate a $1,000 profit on a $50 investment, which is indeed a sizable return for such a small investment. The problem is that the tremendous leverage also involves a high amount of risk, which will most likely result in losses.

The *pattern day trading* rule in the equity market means that traders must maintain at least $25,000 in capital. Even then, this is a relatively small amount of capital to make a living on. Assuming a broker provides 50% margin, which is still only $50,000 to trade in a market where 20% returns are on the high end of the spectrum, still those figures would mean only $10,000 in profit during the first year, which works out to less than $1,000 per month.

In reality, it takes upwards of $250,000 in capital for the most successful day traders to make a living, which is a sizable investment for many retail day traders.

Day Trading on Autopilot

Automated trading systems are commonly advertised throughout the Internet, and they range from the outrageous to the believable. Promoters selling these systems often use deceiving language and statistics to avoid lying, while concealing the problems with their systems.

Suppose that an automated trading system promises a 90% win rate. The high probability of success sounds great at first, but if the average winning trade generates a $5 profit and the average losing trade generates a $50 loss, then the trading system is tremendously unprofitable in spite of the high win rate.

Similarly, suppose that a promoter says he made $684,348 using the automated trading system over the past year. These figures are meaningless given that the initial capital required was not disclosed. If these profits were generated on a $50 million investment, then the rate of return would not be quite as attractive to someone with a $100,000 account.

Even automated trading systems that provide detailed information may not be telling the whole truth. The alleged performance is often from back-testing rather than actual trading, and therefore may not be indicative of future performance. It's quite easy to build a highly successful trading system based only on past performance, since the trading system can be *curve fit* to generate a profit from that data set.

Day traders should avoid automated day trading systems that are developed by third parties, and should instead focus on developing their own systems and techniques. By doing so, they can learn more about how the market works, fully understand how the system functions, and ensure that the trading system's performance is accurately measured.

Personality Cult

James (Jim) Simmons ran what is perhaps the most famous short-term trading operation ever. For more than two decades, his *Renaissance Technologies* hedge fund used trading algorithms to generate annualized returns of around 40%. These algorithms generated a personal fortune estimated at $2.8 billion in 2007 alone. With a background in code breaking with the NSA, Mr. Simmons's biography looks like it was taken straight from a novel.

These success stories have led to a *personality cult* of sorts, where day traders create idealistic images of what the industry is like in their minds. As discussed earlier, the reality is quite different, in that most retail day traders lose money in the long run. Much like entrepreneurs who strike it big and end up with their companies IPO-ing, Mr. Simmons's success, and other success stories like his, are rare.

Returning to the beginning of this section: It is important for traders to set realistic expectations when it comes to day trading. Most novice retail day traders lose money or break even in their first year, and then spend several years working to a point where they can generate a sustainable amount in profit. After several more years, retail day traders may reach a point where they can generate a sustainable income just from day trading alone.

QUICK RECAP

- The stock market provides a unique opportunity to work in a challenging job with potentially unlimited financial upside and flexible working hours, making it an attractive industry for employment as a trader or investor.

- Day traders perceive the stock market as a vehicle for active rather than passive income. They look to make around 20% to 30% per year. Of course, relatively few day traders are actually able to consistently generate 20% to 30% returns each year.

- There are a number of advantages to day trading. One advantage is the ability to consistently take profits out of the business by trading bonuses from brokerages, and the fact that day trading can be done from anywhere in the world as long as there is an Internet connection.

- Day traders face tremendous odds when trading in the stock market, as they have to compete with some of the brightest minds in the world. Furthermore, these competitors have access to more capital and technology, therefore greater economies of scale and a bigger edge.

- Day traders must also deal with many other barriers to entry, such as the high capital requirements of some markets, relatively high commissions as a percentage of total capital, unfair slippage, and the lack of economies of scale.

- The most important consideration before starting a career in day trading is to set the right expectations and ensure that these expectations are in line with real-life needs. New day traders often get sucked into the belief that day trading is both easy and cheap to start pursuing as a career.

- Many myths have been perpetuated in the day trading community. One such myth has to do with the ease of making money and the lack of time commitment needed. In general, individuals would be wise to adhere to the "If it's too good to be true, it probably is" rule.

||||||||||||||||||||||

3

TRADING PSYCHOLOGY

There are many skills that day traders must possess; these skills range from reading charts to calculating risks, though nothing is quite as important as having the right psychology. After all, the majority of short-term trades are dictated by emotion rather than logic. The evidence of these dynamics is clearly seen in the volatility that follows an earnings miss or a brewing economic crisis, instead of a quick and simple one-time revaluation of the security in question.

ARROGANCE

The financial markets humble everyone over time. Sometimes, investors or day traders experience a streak of success and become arrogant. In the end, their overconfidence will be the cause of their downfall. The market's boom-bust cycle reflects these dynamics as investment banks and hedge funds take on excessive risks, only to lose everything eventually, even to the point of requiring a taxpayer bailout. Despite the numerous lessons furnished by past experience, the underlying human psychology persists and history repeats itself. The U.S. housing bubble is just one example; as banks were willing to take on greater risks, credit became increasingly easy to access. The subprime mortgage crisis brought the market back to reality, and credit began to retract as banks looked to reduce their risk and exposure to the market.

These tendencies are known among psychologists as *overconfidence bias*, which means that people tend to have greater confidence in themselves than is warranted. Take the following example: By definition, only half of market participants can be considered above average at any given time, yet a 2006 study of 300 professional fund managers found that 74% thought they had delivered above-average performance, with an additional 26% calling them-selves average. Obviously, it is impossible for these results to be accurate.

A related psychological phenomenon is known as the *hot hand fallacy*. People who have experienced success in a previous event believe they have a greater chance of success in a future event. In the context of day trading, traders may increase their trade sizes after past successes, as they believe they are more likely to experience further success. Their past performance, of course, has nothing to do with future performance, and this fallacy could amplify losses.

Day traders should avoid arrogance and keep their biases in check. The best way to do so is to eliminate these emotions from the process by following a specific set of rules when trading. Another way to avoid these problems is to objectively look at performance on a regular basis and pick a single bench-mark for comparison. For example, a trader may seek to beat the performance of the S&P 500, or reach his own preset target returns.

RULE-BENDING

The single most important part of day trading is following rules, since those rules can eliminate the impact of emotion from the process. Nevertheless, day traders are often tempted to bend the rules in certain situations where they believe they will be able to enhance their profits. The problem with bending the rules is that one's position becomes a lot more uncertain, which means that emotion comes more into play than logic.

Suppose that a trader establishes a position in a stock with a stop-loss set 5% lower than the current market price. After a few minutes, the stock begins to move lower for no apparent reason, and nears the 5% stop-loss level. The trader believes that the stock will turn around and is faced with the choice of removing the stop-loss (in other words, bending the rules a bit), or letting it be triggered for a loss on the position, according to the original rules.

If the trader bends the rules, he is faced with a difficult choice if the stock continues to move lower behind the 5% loss. The lack of a set stop-loss at that point means that the trader could begin to experience the urge to hold the stock even more, so as to recoup the losses. In many cases, these dynamics can lead to steep losses, which, however, are entirely avoidable by sticking to the original plan rather than deviating from it by bending the rules.

DENIAL

The impact of loss—whether it's losing a large sum of money or a loved one—can have devastating effects on the human psyche. In order to protect themselves from the psychological impact, humans have evolved a defense mechanism called *denial*, which allows them to disavow or distort the reality of their situation. Denial in moderation can be useful, but when overused it can become extremely destructive.

Day traders frequently experience losses that can trigger these tendencies, especially because the losses they experience have a greater impact on their livelihood compared to traditional long-term investors or other market participants. In one study where participants gained or lost the same amount of money, the distress experienced from losing money was found to have a greater impact than the joy experienced from gaining money.

Fortunately, there are many strategies that day traders can implement to avoid these problems. The most obvious solution is to establish risk management rules that eliminate the possibility of large losses altogether. In addition to these techniques, day traders should keep a clear record of their trading performance over time, and consistently set aside time to objectively evaluate that performance as a sort of *reality check*.

Aside from avoiding large losses and being cognizant of trading performance, day traders should be honest with their colleagues and family members about their financial situation. It may hurt one's ego to report financial loss, but maintaining a lie amounts to denial.

EMOTIONAL TRADING

Few things cause people as much emotional turmoil as money does. A study conducted by Sonya Britt at the University of Kansas found that disagreements related to money were the primary cause of divorce, regardless of household income level. The impact of money on dopamine is also well established by the gaming industry, which convinces gamblers to hand over huge sums of money in small increments in exchange for the virtually nonexistent possibility of receiving a large payoff.

Day traders face these same emotions on a regular basis in many different ways. As we saw earlier, they must face their own emotional issues when it comes to arrogance or denial or feeling the need to make up for a large loss by making high-risk trades. Day traders must control these emotionally charged situations in order to avoid costly mistakes. Often, the best way to do so is to follow a specific set of predetermined rules when entering and exiting trades, so as to make everything as automated as possible.

The market itself is also largely driven by the aggregate emotion emerging from crowd psychology. In many ways, it's a day trader's job to decipher the market's emotion at any given point in time in order to profit from differences between collective perceptions and reality. News of a product recall may send shares of a manufacturing stock sharply lower, but the real impact of the recall on revenue and profit may be minor and the stock could quickly recover. These types of situation can create significant opportunities to profit.

MANIPULATION

Some professional day traders use deceptive tactics in an attempt to improve their returns, which can make it more difficult for retail traders to compete. For instance, Athena Capital Research paid a $1 million penalty to settle SEC charges after engaging in a practice known as "marking the close," whereby it allegedly manipulated thinly traded stocks in the final two seconds of trading. In an even more prominent case, five major banks—including JPMorgan Chase—paid $3.4 billion in fines for manipulating the currency markets in ways that disadvantaged some of their clients.

Day traders can avoid many types of market manipulation by staying away from illiquid assets. In general, the greater the dollar volume traded each day in a given market, the more costly it becomes to manipulate that market in a meaningful way. Day traders should also shy away from stocks where they have been frequently stopped out, even if those events weren't necessarily caused by provable market manipulation.

There are many cases when the effects of others meddling in the financial markets is unavoidable. For instance, the U.S. Federal Reserve attempted to influence equity prices using unconventional monetary policy in order to restore the public's faith in the market. These announcements led to increased volatility in the equity markets with a bullish skew, which may have been detrimental to day traders with short positions that were otherwise justified by poor fundamentals or technical patterns.

EXECUTION

There are few things in life more exciting than executing a day trade. In addition to the significant amount of money on the line, day traders are actively proving whether or not their intuitions were right or wrong over a period of time. The events surrounding the execution of a trade release dopamine to the brain, possibly clouding one's judgement and leading to costly errors.

If a stock immediately moves lower after a trade is executed, a day trader may question his intuition and be tempted to exit the trade at a loss. This can lead to overtrading, potentially high opportunity costs, and emotional distress for the day trader. Even if a stock moves upward right after a trade is executed, a day trader may become overconfident in his ability to predict stocks, and start to overtrade. This can be even more costly, as there is now a lot more money in questionable trades at risk in the market.

Day traders should focus on developing their trading strategy rather than executing individual trades. When day traders do not let their emotions affect their decisions, the process of executing trades becomes a lot more like a business transaction than pulling the lever of a slot machine. Taken to its extremes, automating the execution of trades can prevent many psychological issues from occurring, and therefore can reduce costly human errors.

DETACHMENT

Detachment is the tendency to deal with anxiety by avoiding situations that can trigger it. In the context of day trading, the phenomenon occurs when traders are hesitant to enter or exit trades as they worry that these trades won't work out. Their hesitation can lead to missed opportunities as well as uncharacteristic trading performance, in the event that the trader acts against a trading system's recommendation.

The easiest way to overcome detachment is to follow a specific set of day trading rules. These rules can help the day trader avoid making emotionally charged decisions. By maintaining the *process-over-profit* mentality, traders won't be tempted to avoid trades. Instead, they will be focused on analyzing the results of the trades and making any necessary changes to their trading rules.

OVERTRADING

By nature day traders place a high number of transactions. Whether via a commission or spread, the costs associated with these transactions can add up quickly.

Overtrading occurs when day traders make an excessive number of transactions in relation to their financial performance. It is often the single most expensive mistake for a novice day trader to make. The mistake is frequently propelled by a combination of *confidence bias*, whereby day traders overestimate their abilities to beat the market, and *compulsive behavior,* whereby day traders strive to take advantage of each and every opportunity that presents itself.

Day traders can avoid overtrading by following a system, the same way that they could avoid the kinds of problems underpinned by rampant emotions. Rather than exploiting every single opportunity that arises, traders can use trading systems to focus on trades with the most favorable risk-reward profiles. These dynamics can help improve the profitability of each trade, and reduce transaction costs over time by making fewer trades.

TRIGGER TROUBLE

Day traders often have trouble pulling the trigger on a trade, since there's often a lot of money on the line. By second-guessing their decisions, *trigger trouble* can lead to worse execution prices and more missed opportunities. These concerns are related to execution issues, whereby a day trader immediately regrets his decision after placing a trade.

Day traders can avoid trigger trouble by building trust into their trading system or strategy. The best way to build trust in these systems is by backtesting with historical data and starting small when executing trades in live markets. Building confidence helps reduce pre-trade anxiety and ensure that trades are executed at the best possible moments. When trading without a specific system, day traders can build their confidence by *paper trading* with fake money in real markets, and then starting small when they first use real capital.

EXITING

Suppose that a day trader established a position that has risen significantly over the past 15 minutes and reached a predetermined exit price. Day traders are often tempted to ditch their plans and let the trade run. The problem with deviating from these plans is that it creates a high level of uncertainty after the exit point is ignored. If the stock moves lower, the day trader may be tempted to try and recoup the losses by holding onto the stock longer. If the stock moves higher, it becomes difficult to pinpoint *any* price at which to lock-in profits.

Day traders can avoid these problems by establishing clear exit points before they even enter a trade. These exit points include both a stop-loss (e.g., the uppermost amount that a trader is willing to lose) and a take-profit (e.g., the point at which they plan to sell). Some day traders who do let profits run may also set up trailing stop-loss points, which automatically adjust higher as a stock price rises so as to lock in profits that fall below the new stop-loss point.

ADDRESSING COMMON ISSUES

Most psychological problems faced by novice day traders can be avoided by adhering to the adage, "plan the trade and trade the plan." In other words, day traders should focus on developing and executing an investment *strategy* rather than executing individual *trades* if they want to avoid making emotionally charged decisions. By doing so, they can focus on the bigger picture and remove as much human error as possible.

Unfortunately, even the best systems experience periods of decline known as *drawdowns*. Most novice day traders will be lucky to break even during their first year. The prospect of losing money or just breaking even after expending a significant amount of effort for an entire year is disheartening to many novice traders. It's therefore important for day traders to develop strong support systems, particularly in the context of family and relationships, which can help them handle these drawdowns. By expecting that they would either lose money or break even, day traders can set the right expectations from the get-go, and focus on improving over the long term so that they may reach their financial goals.

Day traders suffering losses may be tempted to look toward others to provide them with the knowledge or system they need to beat the market. In reality, the skills needed to succeed at day trading are learned skills that become a part of the brain's *basal ganglia,* where instincts are developed. The steep learning curve associated with day trading is a necessary step in the process toward becoming consistently profitable in the market by getting a feel for how the market works.

QUICK RECAP

- Psychology plays a large and underappreciated role in the life of day traders, given the many cognitive biases affecting humans in general. Of course, many of these same biases carry over into the way we behave with money.

- Arrogance in the form of the overconfidence bias can be dangerous, since traders may engage in overtrading or placing trades that aren't well thought out. To avoid it, traders should stick to a specific set of rules when trading.

- Rule bending can be problematic in that it places the day trader in unfamiliar territory. The fix to rule bending is simply to avoid changing the rules under any circumstances and stick to the trading plan.

- Denial is a common and troublesome emotion experienced by many day traders, whereby they fail to acknowledge losses. The best way to avoid falling prey to this is to maintain detailed records and objectively review them every week or month.

- Trading should be a largely nonemotional process, but the involvement of money makes this nearly impossible. As with many of these issues, the solution is to stick to a trading plan and focus on changing the plan instead of changing the trade.

- Traders are often tempted to manipulate a trade after it has been placed against the advice of their trading rules. In many cases, these changes can prove costly and could have been easily avoided by maintaining a hands-off approach.

- Executing trades is oftentimes the most stressful part of day trading, since money is on the line. A common way to avoid execution problems—which could lead to opportunity costs—is to automate trade executing using a trading system.

- Detachment is a common psychological strategy to deal with anxiety, but it can be very costly when it comes to day trading. As with many other things, the best way to avoid detachment is to automate as much of the process as possible.

- Overtrading is a common tendency among day traders, whereby they place an excessive amount of trades due to overconfidence or trying to recoup losses, which can lead to losses and high commission costs over time.

- Trigger trouble happens when day traders have a hard time executing trades without hesitation, which can be avoided by focusing on "following a system" rather than on profiting from each individual transaction.

- Exiting a trade can be tricky for day traders given the tendency to hold onto losers and sell winners quickly, when actually the best course of action is to cut losses short and let winners run in order to maximize risk-adjusted returns over time.

- There are many other important psychological factors that come into play when day-trading, but the good news is, many of them can be avoided by developing a plan and following that plan without making any impulsive changes to it.

WHAT TO TRADE

Day traders can trade in many different markets, whether it be oranges or euros. Each market has its own unique characteristics, advantages, and drawbacks that should be carefully considered before taking the dive. For instance, the large-cap stocks that most day traders focus on will rarely lose their value—a trader will be able to sell them for *something* in the future. On the contrary, an option contract or futures contract loses all its value when the respective agreement expires.

Most markets are known as *derivative markets* where traders buy and sell agreements whose value is derived from the value of an underlying asset. For example, stock options are derivatives that represent the *right* to buy or *obligation* to sell a particular underlying stock at a specified price and time. Their value is derived from the price (or expectations of price change) of the underlying stock, as well as the time remaining on the contract and other factors, rather than intrinsic factors.

For the day trader, the benefit of trading derivatives is *leverage*, which enables him to take on greater risk in exchange for greater returns. Looking back at the stock option example, the right to buy a stock is certainly less than the price of buying the stock outright, but the value of the contract will represent the change in the underlying stock price. The trade-off is that an options trader could lose his entire investment if the stock doesn't reach a certain price.

In this section, we'll examine some of the most common markets as well as the benefits and drawbacks of each that day traders might want to consider.

STOCKS

The stock market is perhaps the most widely known market, which makes it a popular choice for many day traders. In particular, those just getting started with day trading may want to stick to the familiar before branching out into more complex markets.

Stocks represent a percentage ownership in a publicly traded company, which it gives up in order to raise money to finance its growth. Since stocks tend to move higher over time, due to corporations growing in value, the market consists of many long-term investors that buy and hold securities over a long period of time. The reliance on the stock market for household-wealth growth means that it's highly regulated by the government and industry.

A day trader taking advantage of stocks may focus on identifying the top movers on a given day, and then buy and sell those securities based on their volatility. Most opportunities in the stock market are driven by a combination of fundamental events, such as earnings releases or clinical trial results, and technical analysis, such as chart patterns or indicators. Some day traders will also focus on larger indexes using greater amount of leverage to profit.

Advantages of day trading in the stock market include:

- *Highly Regulated* The stock market is regulated by a number of different organizations, including government organization like the U.S. Securities and Exchange Commission (SEC) and independent industry organizations like the Financial Industry Regulatory Authority (FINRA).
- *Highly Liquid* The stock market is generally very liquid, meaning that traders can easily trade in and out of stocks, although there are many areas of the stock market where liquidity isn't as readily available, such as ADRs or OTC stocks.

- *Upward Bias* The stock market has increased in value over time, unlike many other asset classes, since corporate valuations have trended upward. In fact, the S&P 500 index has averaged a 12% annual return since its inception.
- *Well-Studied* The stock market has been widely studied by academics, economists, and analysts, which means that day traders have access to a lot of tools and information that can be used to improve trading performance.

Disadvantages of day trading stocks include:

- *High Requirements* Day traders must start with and maintain a minimum $25,000 balance if they are classified as pattern day traders, which is a sizable sum of money for many novice day traders just getting started.
- *Low Leverage* Day traders using margin accounts have access to 50% leverage under Regulation T ("Reg T"), which is significantly less than many other markets that offer leverage of up to 50-to-1 or greater.

FUTURES

The futures market is perhaps the most widely-traded market for professional day traders, given the increased leverage available compared to the stock market. However, novice day traders should tread carefully in this market, given the added risks that it entails.

Futures contracts are derivatives specifying that an underlying asset will be bought or sold for a specific price on a specific date in the future. These assets may include equity indexes like the S&P 500, commodities like crude oil, or nearly any other type of asset. In general, the futures market consists of commercial hedgers trying to ensure they receive a certain price for their product, and speculators that try to profit from changes in the underlying assets.

For instance, a farmer may be growing a large quantity of wheat and wish to ensure that he receives a certain price for the harvest next year. The farmer may sell a futures contract to lock in that price to a speculator that believes wheat prices are headed higher. When the delivery date approaches, the speculator may sell his contract to a cereal manufacturer, who will then take physical delivery of the wheat and realize a profit on the sale.

The futures market also has its own set of industry jargon that novice traders should know. For instance, the tendency of the price of a futures contract to move toward the price of its underlying asset over time is known as *convergence*. When a futures price is higher than the spot price of a commodity, the futures contract is said to be in *contango*, while a spot price higher than a futures price is known as *backwardation*. These terms may seem foreign when just getting started, but they will quickly become familiar over time.

There are many advantages to trading futures:

- *Greater Leverage* The futures market provides day traders with greater leverage, enabling them to put up very little margin. For instance, equity index futures involve as little as 10% of the contract's total value as margin.
- *Low Cost* The commissions paid on futures contracts are often smaller than the commissions paid on stocks and other assets.
- *No Restrictions* The futures market has fewer restrictions than the equity markets, including lower minimum capital requirements.[10]

There are also some disadvantages to trading futures:

- *No Bias* Futures contracts are short-term investments that don't have the same upward bias as equities, which can make them more difficult to predict.
- *Greater Volatility* The futures market is much more volatile than the equity markets given the higher amount of leverage, which makes it riskier for day traders.

OPTIONS

Day traders often use the options market to increase leverage or hedge positions in the equities and other markets. However, options can be risky for novice day traders, with the potential of losing their entire investment.

Options are derivative contracts that provide the right to buy or sell an underlying asset at a specific price and time in the future. When buying options, traders are purchasing the rights to an underlying asset. When selling (or writing) options, traders are selling the rights to the underlying asset.

Naked positions occur when a trader sells the right to an underlying asset without actually owning that asset.

Many options are considered high-risk because they are significantly more volatile than the underlying asset, and almost always have less liquidity. As an options contract approaches expiration, it may also be at high risk of complete loss. For example, a contract to buy a stock at $10.00 that expires at the end of the day could be worthless if the underlying stock doesn't rise above $10.00 per share, but could be worth a lot if it does do so.

Advantages to trading options include:

- *Leverage* Options provide day traders with greater leverage, since they represent the rights to an underlying asset instead of the assets themselves.
- *Protection* Options enable day traders to hedge existing positions to reduce the risk to their portfolios at any given point in time.

Disadvantages of trading options include:

- *Lack of Liquidity* Many options have significantly less liquidity than the equities underlying them, which can make it difficult to buy and sell the assets.
- *Risk of Complete Loss* Options can expire and become completely worthless if an underlying asset doesn't reach the desired price before a specified time.

CURRENCIES

The foreign exchange market—also known as the currency or *forex* market—is the largest and most liquid market in the world. The amount of money running through the forex market every day has been estimated to be between $2 trillion and $4 trillion. Day traders may also appreciate that the market is open 24 hours a day, six days a week!

Trading currencies involves simultaneously buying one currency and selling another in so-called *currency pairs*. The most widely traded currency pair is the euro–U.S. dollar, or EUR/USD. Purchasing the EUR/USD currency pair involves using U.S. dollars to purchase euros and then profiting when they are converted back. If the euro appreciated in value, the trader would be able to repurchase the same amount of euros for fewer U.S. dollars.

Day traders active in the currency markets use a significant amount of leverage in order to profit from such small daily price movements. In the absence of fundamental changes or changes in the perception of national economies, the market is largely driven by technical analysis and the activities of very large institutional traders. The combination of high leverage and a lack of regulations make the industry relatively risky for smaller retail day traders, since margin is a double-edged sword and loose regulations provide very little retail protection.

Advantages of trading currencies include:

- *Liquidity* The forex market is the largest and most liquid market in the world, which means that traders will never have any trouble entering and exiting trades.
- *Leverage* The forex market isn't very highly regulated and high leverage is available for traders that dare to use it, which means profit potential is enormous.
- *No Commissions* Forex brokers generate their cut from the spread rather than by charging outright commissions on each trade.

Disadvantages of trading currencies include:

- *Lack of Regulation* The forex market lacks many of the regulatory controls enjoyed by the equity markets, which means that traders face greater risk.
- *Volatility* The forex market is characterized by high levels of volatility, which makes it much more risky than many other asset classes.

BONDS

The bond market is not nearly as popular as equities or futures among day traders, but as other markets become more competitive, it has become increasingly attractive.

Bonds are asset-backed (or tax-backed) debt instruments issued by governments or corporations that may or may not involve interest payments. Since prevailing interest rates and risk factors are constantly changing, the price of bonds tends to fluctuate over time. Some bonds—such as *junk bonds*—are exceptionally volatile given their already-high risk profile, creating an opportunity to realize high yields even when compared to equities.

Advantages of trading bonds include:

- *Macro Trades* Trading in government bonds, like Treasuries, is essentially a bet on interest rates, which makes them great for short-term macro-economic bets.
- *Alternative Asset Class* Bonds are relatively uncorrelated with equities, making them a great alternative when equities are difficult to trade. Diversification helps reduce non-systematic risks by shielding an entire portfolio from losses associated with a single asset class.

Disadvantages of trading bonds include:

- *Less Liquidity* Corporate bonds don't have nearly as much liquidity as equities, which can make them difficult to buy and sell on short notice.
- *Less Leverage* Day traders have less access to leverage in the bond market compared to other markets, like currencies, futures, or equities.

CONTRACTS FOR DIFFERENCE (CFDs)

The market for Contracts for Difference is great for betting on the solvency of a government or corporation. Day traders often use CFDs as a hedge for other assets, especially during difficult times.

Contracts for Difference are agreements between two parties to exchange the difference between the opening and closing price for a specified asset. In essence, CFDs enable day traders to bet on a price movement without actually purchasing the underlying asset. For example, a day trader may believe shares of Acme Co. are going to fall from $100 to $95. A CFD would enable the trader to put up just 20% of the $100 ($20) and realize the same $5 gain, which represents a 25% gain instead of a 5% gain by purchasing the stock.

Advantages of trading CFDs include:

- *Simple* CFDs are relatively straightforward derivatives that enable day traders to leverage their exposure to a given asset.
- *Leveraged* CFDs offer a high level of leverage compared to many other asset types, with the ability to only put 10% or 20% down.

Disadvantages of trading CFDs include:

- *Higher Risk* CFDs involve a high level of risk compared to traditional assets, since the day trader can realize a complete loss in a short period of time due to the use of leverage. After all, leverage is a double-edged sword that amplifies both gains and losses.
- *Counterparty Risk* The CFD market is not very regulated compared to many other assets, which introduces counterparty risk.

QUICK RECAP

- There are many different types of assets for day traders to consider, but it's important to understand the mechanics, benefits, and drawbacks of these assets. Different assets have different risk profiles and start-up requirements.

- Stocks represent the most popular class of assets for many day traders because of their high liquidity, tight regulation, and upward bias. In general, most day traders begin their careers in the stock market and then move into other markets later on.

- Commodities represent the second most popular class of assets for day traders, because of their high liquidity and significant volatility due to weather patterns, seasonality, and other factors. Day traders looking for greater volatility will look toward these markets for opportunities.

- Currencies represent the single largest and most liquid market in the world, with trillions of dollars changing hands every day. While the market has limited oversight, it's becoming increasingly popular for many day traders.

- Bonds represent a small and growing portion of the retail day trading market that is driven by those taking advantage of government bonds. With increased volatility in recent years, the market is becoming increasingly popular among day traders.

- CFDs are a relatively new type of derivative in the financial markets. They provide a unique risk/reward profile compared to traditional assets. Most day traders stay away from this asset class due to its lack of regulation and higher risk.

TOOLS OF THE TRADE

There are several requirements for day traders before getting started in the profession, ranging from having enough time and money to having the right kind of brokerage account. While it's possible to dabble in trading without some of these things—such as sufficient starting capital—doing so is usually unsustainable and may result in quick losses. The key to success is practicing paper trading with a demo account using the same tools as you'd be using in a live account, and then slowly transitioning to the live account with adequate capital and the right tools in place.

In this section, we'll explore some of the core tools necessary to getting started on day trading.

MONEY

Money is the single most important resource for day traders. Without adequate funds, traders must take on more risk to realize sufficient returns.

These risks translate to lower risk-adjusted returns over time, as costly mistakes eat away at returns. Day traders should try to maximize their available funds in order to reduce these risks and improve their risk-adjusted returns, taking into account that stretching a personal financial budget entails its own problems.

By committing a high percentage of their total net worth, day traders risk increasing their emotional investment in the venture. Such emotional investment could be detrimental to trading performance (the reasons for which we have discussed earlier in the book). When more is at stake, day traders are more prone to making costly mistakes. These mistakes can be avoided by ensuring that only a comfortable portion of total net worth is invested in the venture.

Aside from their cash investment in the venture, day traders have access to many different margin opportunities, depending on the markets they're targeting. Most stock market brokers provide leverage of up to 50%, which means that a day trader with a $50,000 account may actually have access to $75,000 in trading capital. When margin is used, the trade is charged an interest rate on the borrowed money and the broker may issue a *margin call* when the margin posed in the account is below the minimum margin requirement.

The law requires that equity market day traders maintain a minimum $25,000 account balance at all times, but many other markets don't have the same limitations. For instance, day traders can start with as little as $100 in the forex market, which can be leveraged at 100-to-1 or greater to effectively trade with $10,000 worth of capital. The tradeoff is that leverage entails greater risk. If a $10,000 trade loses just 1% of its value, the broker could issue a margin call and the day trader will lose his $100 investment.

Many proprietary trading (or *prop trading*) firms provide day traders with an alternative source of capital. In exchange for profit-sharing and adhering to other conditions, prop traders have access to a limited amount of institutional capital in addition to their own capital.

MARGIN

Suppose that you're playing poker at a casino and are running low on funds. With your luck starting to turn around, your friend decides to spot you an extra $100 to stay in the game, provided that you give her $125 in return. Your luck does start to turn around and you end up pocketing $500 for the night, even after paying your friend back the full $125. In that case, the borrowed money helped facilitate the profit, but it could just as easily have led to a loss that was amplified by $125. These dynamics are similar to *margin trading*.

Margin is an important concept for day traders to understand, since it's both required for pattern day traders and highly useful for leveraging trades. If used properly, margin can help improve profitability by using borrowed money to trade. The catch is that margin is a double-edged sword and can quickly compound losses if used improperly. Since day trading involves capitalizing on small and rapid price movements, margin is a tool that nearly every day trader will need to familiarize himself or herself with over time.

Margin Mechanics

Day traders have access to up to 50% margin when trading U.S. stocks within a margin account, meaning they can borrow up to 50% of their account value. After making the purchase on margin, traders can keep the loan as long as they would like, provided that the obligations—including repayment and interest—are fulfilled. The loan is repaid in full when the position is sold, before any of the proceeds are distributed to the trader.

The biggest risk associated with trading on margin is the dreaded *margin call*. Within a margin account, brokers require a minimum *maintenance margin*, or minimum account balance to be maintained, otherwise they force a trader to either deposit more money or sell the stock to pay down the loan. The minimum maintenance margin required by law is 25%, but individual brokers may have more specific requirements. A *margin call* occurs when the broker demands additional cash to be deposited or that the securities be sold.

A final important consideration is that, over time, interest accrues on margin; hence the break-even point is constantly increasing. While the interest usually accrues as a payable on the account, traders may make the payments in cash to brokers if they so wish. These dynamics mean that margin accounts are usually only practical to use for short-term traders—like day traders—rather than long-term investors.

Advantages & Disadvantages

There are many advantages and disadvantages to using margin. To illustrate these examples, let's take a look at two scenarios showing what happens when margin has a positive effect and what happens when problems arise.

First, let's take a look at how margin can help improve trading performance.

Suppose that a day trader wishes to buy $5,000 worth of a stock that's trading at $10.00 per share with a price target of $11.00 per share. If the trader simply used his own capital, the trade would produce a 10% profit or $500 on a $5,000 investment. The trader could improve these performance metrics by trading on margin. If a broker provides up to 50% margin, the trader could borrow $2,500 and use only $2,500 of his own capital in the trade. These dynamics would equate to a $500 gain on a $2,500 investment—or a 20% profit, where the other $2,500 in the account could be used in other promising trades.

Now, let's take a look at the risks associated with trading on margin.

Suppose the same day trader buys the same stock, but instead of increasing to $11.00 per share, the stock falls to $9.00 per share. In this case, the trader lost $500 on a $2,500 investment—or a 20% decline—when using margin. The bigger problem occurs when a broker decides that the trade is too risky and demands to be repaid in what's known as a *margin call*. When this occurs, the trader must either put up the additional margin—in this case, $2,500 in cash—or the entire position will be sold for a loss. The latter scenario can lead to significant losses, particularly when the day trader can't afford to put up the extra margin.

In the end, margin is an invaluable tool that day traders can use to amplify their gains, but they should be careful when using it, since it's a double-edged sword in many ways.

TIME

The only other major requirement for day traders is time. While some retail day traders try to trade part-time, those looking to achieve the highest chances of success should consider committing to trading as a full-time profession. There are many different ways to go about becoming a full-time day trader, including working for yourself or someone else. Would-be day traders should carefully consider these options before deciding what is best suited for their situation, and set themselves the right expectations from the start.

Part-Time vs. Full-Time

A key decision that novice day traders must make is whether to pursue day trading as a full-time or part-time job.

As a part-time job, day trading may involve trading equities on certain days off, or trading currencies during non-business hours. A great example may be someone who enjoys trading on his days off in order to make some extra money. Given the high starting capital requirements in some markets, like U.S. equities, these traders may focus on futures or other markets that are less restrictive and/or have longer hours. The trade-off is that part-time day traders shouldn't expect to make as much or perform as well as full-time traders.

As a full-time job, day trading involves working from pre-market to post-market hours and perhaps longer, in order to obtain returns sufficient for sustaining a decent quality of life. An example would be a day trader who takes a job working with a prop trading firm in order to learn the ropes, and then slowly begins to trade his own capital over time as he is able to pay the bills and generate more consistent returns. The trade-off is that full-time day trading is a very difficult and risky job that's much more difficult to master.

Alone vs. Prop Trading

A second decision that must be made is whether to join a prop trading firm or venture out on your own. With access to institutional capital and educational resources, prop trading is an attractive way to get started in day trading without the high capital investment. The trade-off is that a large portion of profit goes to the prop trading firm, and there are sometimes other costs involved with working at these firms, such as commission and educational fees. Some firms even charge day traders to become involved. Traders should do their research on a firm before taking the plunge and joining them.

The decision to go it alone has its own advantages and disadvantages. With the significant upfront capital costs, day trading can introduce a lot of financial-related stress into someone's life and is quite difficult to master. The obvious advantages are that the trader controls his own destiny, doesn't have to pay out any profits to third parties, and ultimately profits the most from his own performance.

DIRECT ACCESS TRADING

Direct Access Trading enables day traders to transact directly with exchanges rather than going through intermediaries like stockbrokers. With a direct connection to exchanges, these accounts benefit from faster transaction speeds, reduced slippage, and reduced expenses compared to traditional intermediaries. The accounts may also permit day traders to route their own orders to specific market makers to achieve desired outcomes.

The average direct access trading account pays a commission based on the number of shares traded rather than the number of transactions. In the equity market, these figures amount to around $0.005 per share, which is significantly less than traditional stock brokers that may charge $9.99 for a single trade. Scalpers or other day traders that trade greater volumes of stock may also qualify for further discounts from these rates.

Direct access trading accounts usually require a minimum investment that varies depending on the provider, and a minimum activity level. For example, a broker might require a $10,000 minimum to open an account and then at least $30 per month in commissions to avoid monthly fees. If the minimum activity isn't met, day traders may face inactivity fees or other consequences. Novice day traders should also familiarize themselves with the many differences between traditional brokers and direct access trading accounts in order to avoid any accidents or errors when trading.

BUSINESS PLAN

The first step to getting started in day trading is to establish a business plan to ensure revenue is sufficient, expenses are contained, and the tax implications of day trading are fully accounted for beforehand. Business plans can also help day traders set goals and outline how they will be achieved on paper, providing them with the same benefits that entrepreneurs realize from putting their goals and plans into writing for banks and investors.

When writing a business plan, the first thing to think about may be the amount of money required each month. Full-time day traders may require $5,000 per month in gross income, while part-time traders may be more flexible with their financial needs. These figures provide a great starting point to determine whether or not their goals are reasonable, and ultimately help determine how much starting capital will be required to reach them.

For example, suppose that a day trader wishes to make $2,000 per month or roughly $24,000 per year. Knowing that a good year would yield 20% returns, the trader may estimate they will make 15%, which would mean they would need $160,000 in starting capital. They may be able to borrow 50% of that total on margin, which means the total they would need to come up with out of pocket may be closer to $107,000 after all is said and done.

The next step is establishing a firm capital-and-time commitment to day trading based on the assumptions made in the earlier steps. When making these considerations, it's important for day traders to consider whether they will be using their own capital or trade on behalf of a proprietary trading firm to reduce their personal risk. The amount of time dedicated to day trading should also correlate with the desired return on invested capital.

After establishing these parameters, the next step is documenting some of the day-to-day tools and methods that will be used. Record keeping, performance reviews, and tax reporting are three important areas under this umbrella that should be carefully considered. Many brokers offer automated record-keeping tools, as well as performance analytics, but day traders should check with their accountants to ensure these records are sufficient. Traders should also carefully think about how often performance metrics should be checked and how to address any potential problems with performance.

The core of the business plan should consist of the trading strategies and risk management techniques that will be used to generate consistent returns. In this section, day traders should provide specific details concerning their trading rules and past performance either in the live market (ideally), or when backtesting. The amount of leverage applied for and used when trading should also be specified in this section. Risk management rules should also be spelled out in detail, including default stop-loss levels, maximum drawdowns, and other rules to follow when trading systems do not perform as expected.

Finally, the business plan should include some compensation details. For example, day traders may specify how much money they intend to take out of the business as a salary and how much they will leave in the business to enhance future returns. These figures are important for setting expectations in times of success and failure.

LEVEL II QUOTES

The original "day trader" used ticker tape as his primary source of information. After stock trades were executed, they would be recorded and transmitted by telegraph to traders, who would receive printouts known as *ticker tape* through a *stock ticker* machine. The readings would include the *ticker symbol*, execution price, and number of shares transacted. These readings provided key insights into where traders and investors were putting their capital.

Modern stock quotes are delivered electronically through brokers or other financial data providers. The real-time ticker on the bottom of CNBC's cable television show indicates the latest transactions occurring in popular stocks for the day. While most traders view quotes through their broker platforms at the time of purchase, these external real-time stock tickers are used to highlight how news and events are affecting stocks in the moment.

In addition to the latest trades, day traders have access to a plethora of other data points, including the complete *order book* for a stock. The order book contains all of the outstanding limit orders on both the bid-side and ask-side of the trade. For example, the bid-side of an order book may have an entry stating 1.43 × 200, which indicates that there's a limit order to buy 200 shares of stock at $1.43 per share.

A trade is executed when a bid is matched to an ask within an order book for a set number of shares. After the trade is executed, the transaction will appear on the time and sales data feed, and the latest price of the stock will be updated everywhere. These simple transactions dictate how stock prices move over time, driven by the constant matching of bid and ask prices from an order book.

Some day traders believe that the only information necessary to trade in the short-term is the order book. By looking at the sizes of orders at various prices, they can identify areas of support and resistance for prices. Traders can also gauge the momentum of a stock by looking at where the large block orders are being placed relative to smaller block orders, where a *block* represents the number of shares being traded.

Levels of Quotes

There are four "levels" of stock quotes available within the market:

- *Level I* Level I quotes provide a basic real-time quote that shows the latest price and the closest bid/ask prices and levels to that price. For example, a Level I quote may show a current price of 9.89 per share, a bid of 9.88 × 100, and an ask of 9.90 × 200.
- *Level II* Level II quotes provide a look into a complete order book where a trader can see a complete list of open limit orders on both the bid-side and ask-side. These quotes are broken down based on the *market maker* that's providing the quote.
- *TotalView* The NASDAQ's TotalView goes a step further than Level II quotes by offering more market depth and by grouping various orders by market participant in order to get a clearer picture of who stands where.

- *Level III* Level III quotes are restricted to NASD member firms, providing all of the functionality of Level I and Level II quotes with the additional ability to change orders and send information. As a result, these quotes usually don't apply to retail day traders.

Reading Quotes

Level II quotes are the most popular type of quotes used by retail day traders. While some brokers provide free Level II access, others may charge extra for the option to see these quotes in real-time. In basic terms, these quotes are useful when determining the strength of support and resistance levels by looking at open orders around those prices. So-called *depth charts* can visually show where the largest open limit orders are concentrated.

In Figure 1, the left column represents bid orders, or buyers, and the right column represents ask orders, or sellers. In each column, traders can find the market maker responsible for the order, the limit price for the order to be

Bid	Size	Time	MMID	Ask	Size	
617.77	1	10:54:04	baty	617.87	1	10:
617.60	1	10:54:04	edga	617.87	1	10:
617.60	1	10:54:01	NSDQ	617.88	1	10:
617.51	1	10:53:52	bats	617.92	4	10:
617.50	3	10:53:51	edgx	618.05	1	10:
617.50	1	10:51:39	arcx	618.36	1	10:
617.50	1	10:54:04	UBSS	618.40	1	10:
617.43	2	10:54:02	amex	618.40	1	10:
616.93	1	10:53:59	WCHV	618.50	1	10:
616.60	1	10:54:05	cinn	618.50	1	10:
616.59	1	10:53:52	HDSN	618.81	1	10:
616.32	1	08:30:36	bosx	618.87	1	10:
615.37	1	10:53:52	NITE	620.13	1	08:
611.51	1	06:56:45	cbsx	624.02	1	06:
611.49	1	08:33:23	NMRA	624.93	1	08:
611.00	1	05:29:01	SBSH	625.00	1	10:
603.61	1	07:24:09	SUSQ	631.05	1	07:
603.00	1	07:02:27	MSCO	633.21	1	10:

Figure 1. Level II Depth Chart. Source: eSignal.com

DAY TRADING

executed at, and the quantity of shares associated with the order. The areas with large blocks of bid or ask shares represent the key areas that day traders should watch in conjunction with the support and resistance levels seen on stock charts.

Market makers are identified by a four-letter abbreviation, with many of them associated with a certain brokerage firm or other entity participating in the financial markets. In general, market makers can be divided into either wholesale trades, retail trades, or ECNs, where wholesale trades are those placed by institutional traders, retail trades are those placed by retail brokers, and ECNs are simply electronic networks that handle either type of trade.

Some common market makers are:

- NITE Knight Securities
- SCHB UBS Capital Markets
- TDCM TD Waterhouse
- ETRD eTrade Capital Markets
- ARCA Archipelago

The largest market maker in a given security that's controlling the action is known as the *Ax* in day trading circles, although they aren't always present in a given stock. In general, day traders should pay attention to the direction that the Ax is pushing prices in order to ensure that they are on the right side of the trade. However, the Ax may also route orders to ECNs, in order to avoid publishing their trades under their normal market maker code.

It is also important to realize that trades do not have to go through these venues and be reported. While there's a risk that some orders aren't showing up on Level II order books, many large institutional traders will advertise their bid and ask orders in order to make executing them easier. The reality is that unadvertised orders do not have a significant impact on the market, since they consist largely of smaller block sizes.

What to Watch

Level II quotes provide a lot of different insights for day traders to use when deciding whether or not to buy a stock.

Some traders prefer to use Level II quotes and the order book as their primary source of information when placing trades. For instance, traders may identify a trading range based on big block orders at a certain bid and ask price. Within that range, traders may focus on making trades along with the largest blocks at the time until the price approaches the resistance level, and then exit the position. The trader may also use insights gleaned from *which* market makers are placing the orders by differentiating between stronger institutional accounts and weaker retail accounts.

In addition to providing on-the-spot insights to day traders, Level II quotes and order books can be used within trading systems to improve the odds of a successful trade by incorporating a greater amount of information about the market. A trader might qualify support and resistance levels by looking at market depth charts at those prices. If a trader finds a support level with no substantial bid orders supporting it, he might put in a greater number of safeguards in order to protect against a breakdown that may be more likely to occur under these market circumstances.

In either case, the most important thing that Level II quotes do is provide a confirmation of support or resistance levels by showing where large blocks of shares are placed. For instance, if a stock recently began falling from its highs and a large block stands at a bid price of 2.00, day traders can assume that 2.00 will be the next major support level.

Important dynamics to watch:

- *Market Makers* Market makers may exhibit certain trading patterns that day traders can recognize and profit from over time. Oftentimes, day traders will watch the market makers in a given stock over time and get a feel for how they act throughout the day.
- *Depth Chart* The depth chart shows where the largest volume is concentrated in terms of price in order to show areas of potential support and resistance. By using these levels, day traders can validate chart patterns or other indicators.
- *Intentions* Institutional traders and other traders in the market may place bid and ask orders without ever intending to execute them, just so they can spook other traders in the market into taking action. They can then get

their other orders filled at a good price. Day traders who understand these dynamics can use them to their advantage.

Risks & Other Considerations

Level II quotes are a great way for day traders to gain additional insights into the forces behind price changes over time, but the quotes should be taken with a grain of salt because it's possible for a lot of the true story to be masked. For example, a large trader could route his trades through an ECN to disguise the source of the trades, which makes it difficult to confirm or deny that a single larger buyer is accumulating a stock.

Traders may also place orders that are never meant to be executed in order to trick others in the market. These are known as *ghosts,* and could either be indicative of a large trader changing his mind, or someone trying to drum up support without putting the capital behind it. The only way to confirm that an order is executed is to cross-check it against the time and sales data feed by looking for similar block sizes that have been executed.

In the end, Level II quotes and order books are a vital source of information for day traders, since they provide a lot of additional information to support other forms of technical analysis.

QUICK RECAP

- Capital is the single largest requirement for day traders, with at least $25,000 in starting capital required for pattern day traders in U.S. equity markets. In general, most day traders use margin to leverage their positions by up to 50%.

- Time is the second largest requirement for day traders. While part-time day trading is a possibility, the most successful traders devote themselves full-time to the profession. Proprietary trading may also offer a path to full-time involvement for many beginners.

- A comprehensive business plan is a great way to set expectations and think through a career decision before making the jump. These plans should include as much information as possible and take into account all possible risk factors.

- Direct access trading accounts are ideal because they lower cost for high-volume day trading compared to traditional brokerage accounts. Execution times are also improved, since traders are interacting directly with exchanges.

- Day traders write and follow a detailed business plan that includes how much they plan to invest and how much they anticipate making. By doing so, traders can help set the right expectations from the start and improve the odds of success over the long-term.

- Level II quotes represent a final requirement for day traders, since they provide real-time insights into price movements. By examining these quotes, traders can discern what prices have the highest amount of volume associated with them.

6

‖‖‖‖‖‖‖‖‖‖‖‖‖‖‖‖‖‖

CHARTING & PATTERNS

Suppose you are asked to summarize demographics data consisting of millions of individual data points across a large geographical area. Of course, showing a giant spreadsheet on a projector won't be of much use to an audience, since they are not capable of discerning any trends just by looking at numbers. A better option might be to create a pie chart or line charts, in order to visualize the data and make it more palatable for the audience. By doing so, the audience will be able to instantly understand the key points before digging deeper.

Charts are the single most important resource for many day traders, because they provide these types of high-level insights into the market's psychology. At a glance, they can help evaluate whether a security is trending higher or lower, whether investors are confident or nervous, and what levels are being watched most closely. Technical analysts believe that prices and charts reflect all publicly available information at a given time, which makes them one of the few resources that are truly necessary in order to make trading decisions.

Day traders use charts to determine whether they should buy or sell, identify ideal entry and exit points for their positions, and ultimately improve the odds of placing a successful trade. Since they are focused on intraday price movements, the insights that charts provide are far more valuable than fundamental analysis-related insights that may take months or years to be reflected in an asset's price. Those proficient in chart analysis can pinpoint when an asset's price is about to break out, break down, or experience sideways trading.

There are many different types of charts that reflect price patterns in different ways, making it possible to see them in a different light. For instance, a standard *bar chart* (discussed below) shows the open, high, low, and closing price of a security over a period of time, while *point and figure charts* ignore time and focus only on trend changes. Day traders can also examine the same type of charts across different timeframes to gain broad context. For example, a stock that's trending higher in a 1-minute chart may be doing so in the context of a steep decline in the 1-year chart, which means that a breakout may not be as durable.

Charts can be analyzed and extended in many different ways. By looking at price patterns, day traders can identify potential opportunities in the form of support or resistance levels. Technical indicators can be overlaid on charts to provide visual insights into statistical analysis performed on prices over time, too. For instance, a moving average can be overlaid on a chart showing the current average of the past 50 days' worth of prices. These levels may act as support or resistance levels of their own, if the market heavily watches them.

The study of charts constitutes a significant portion of technical analysis, which makes them extremely important for day traders to understand. By reading charts every day, traders can become proficient in using them to identify promising opportunities and enhance their chances of making successful trades.

TIMEFRAMES

The stereotypical day trader sits in front of four or five monitors with each of them showing actively moving charts and data feeds. While the need for many monitors is somewhat of a myth, many day traders do utilize a lot of different charts for the same stock or asset in order to gain greater perspective into the price action. This perspective comes from looking at different timeframes for the same stock, much like a traveler can zoom out on a map for greater perspective of where they are within a city or country.

For instance, an intraday one-minute chart may show that a stock has been heading higher over the past hour or two. A day trader who bases his decision solely on this chart might be tempted to buy the stock. But after zooming out to the 52-week one-day chart, the trader may find that the same stock is the midst of a significant downturn. These new revelations might suggest that the stock is undergoing a *dead cat bounce* and may be headed lower soon, which could lead to the trader short-selling the stock—the exact opposite conclusion.

Day traders may also use multiple timeframes to establish many different levels of support and resistance. For example, a long-term chart may show a significant resistance level from a prior high that doesn't necessarily appear on a short-term chart. These levels are important, since longer-term support and resistance tends to be much stronger than shorter-term support and resistance, given that they have been touched more frequently.

Charts consist of various ticks with each tick representing a given unit of time, and most day traders like to look at multiple timeframes when making decisions. For instance, an intraday one-minute chart shows the up-to-the-second price movements that are integral to day trading, but a one-year chart with each tick representing one day shows a better longer-term overall picture. The benefit of the big picture is that day traders can ensure they're trading with the trend, and they may be able to better identify support and resistance levels.

Most day traders prefer to have at least two charts, with one showing one-minute data on an intraday chart, and one longer-term chart that may be one-day or one-hour ticks over the course of a year. Of course, the exact timeframes used will depend on the situation.

BAR CHARTS

Bar charts are the most popular type of chart used by both long-term investors and short-term traders. Using high, low, and closing price data, the
standard bar chart consists of a vertical line representing the distance
between the low and high for the day, with a short horizontal line showing
the closing price. Bar charts enable traders to quickly determine whether
the price closed near its high or low for the period, which can be an indicator
of the market's confidence and help predict where prices may be headed in
the future.

So-called *OHLC bar charts* are a popular variant of the standard bar chart
that show both the opening and closing prices rather than just the closing
price. In these charts, there is a small horizontal line to the left of the vertical line showing the opening price and a small horizontal line to the right of
the vertical line showing the closing price. The benefit of showing the opening price is that day traders can get a much clearer idea of whether the stock
moved higher or lower and where it closed relative to the closing price.

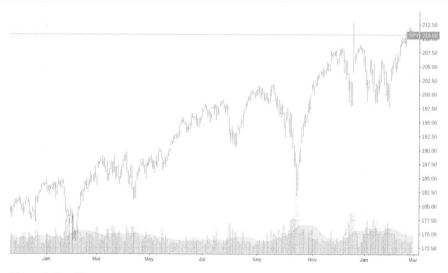

Figure 2. Bar Chart

A key benefit of using bar charts is the ability to show a lot of data in a limited amount of space. Unlike candlestick charts, bar charts do not appear cluttered when a large number of data points are shown on the same chart and scrunched together. And unlike *line charts* that only plot closing prices, bar charts provide a glimpse into price volatility by showing the difference between the high and low for each period. These dynamics make the bar chart an excellent choice when looking to fit the greatest number of ticks into a given timeframe.

The corollary is that bar charts do two things only half as good as other alternatives: When traders are looking for detailed insights, candlestick charts provide a much clearer picture of what happened during the period; and when looking for clear-cut trends, line charts provide a smoother representation of where prices are headed. Bar charts compromise in both of these areas to provide a middle ground for day traders, which can be useful in some situations but may be a hindrance in others.

CANDLESTICK CHARTS

Candlestick charts have become extremely popular since their introduction in Japan over 300 years ago. Like bar charts, candlestick charts use open, high, low, and close data to create insightful visualizations to help day traders better evaluate a stock.

The key difference between a candlestick chart and bar chart is the way each tick is represented. Whereas bar charts are simply vertical and horizontal lines, candlestick charts consist of *candles* that have a thick rectangle ("body") and protruding vertical lines ("shadows" or "tails"). The body of a candle represents the difference between the opening and closing price with a different color, depending on whether the closing price was above or below the opening price. As with bar charts, the vertical lines represent the period's trading range by covering the distance between the high and low.

Technical analysts pay closest attention to the body of a candle, since its shape and patterns can tell an important story. For example, a small body

Figure 3. Candlestick Chart

and short tails produce a candle that look like a lot like a plus sign ("+"). These candles are known as *doji stars* and indicate indecision in the market, which suggests a potential reversal in the price trend. Multiple candles may also form patterns that yield useful insights. For instance, a large candle body that completely covers—or engulfs—the following candle is known as an *engulfing* and also indicates a potential reversal, since the power is shifting between bulls and bears.

Some important candlestick chart patterns to know are:

- *Doji Stars* Doji stars patterns occur when the opening and closing price are equal or very close to equal, while the upper and low shadows may vary. The pattern is indicative of a high level of indecision in the market, with the direction of the tails pointing toward the bullish or bearish bias seen during the period.

- *Hammers* Hammer patterns occur when the opening and closing prices are relatively close to each other with a long upper or lower shadow, which results in a candle that resembles a hammer (or inverted hammer). The pattern indicates a likely reversal in price when it occurs near the top or bottom of a downward or upward price trend.

- *Engulfings* Engulfing patterns occur when one candle is completely eclipsed by the following candle, including its tails. When this happens, it's usually a sign that the price is about to move in the direction of the second candle, whether it's a reversal of a trend or a continuation of an existing trend.
- *Harami* Harami patterns are the opposite of an engulfing, when the first candle entirely eclipses the second candle, which indicates that the price is likely to move in the same direction as the second candle predicts. The pattern usually occurs at the top or bottom of a long-term trend and acts as a reversal indicator.

Candlestick charts are most useful for making snap decisions. While chart patterns and technical indicators show potential upcoming continuations or reversals over the course of hours or days, candlesticks predict movement within the next few ticks. For example, an ascending triangle pattern and a bullish MACD crossover may suggest that a breakout is possible in the near future, but a day trader may actually pull the trigger when they see a bullish engulfing candlestick pattern suggesting very near-term upside.

The only major shortcoming of candlestick charts is that they don't reflect intraperiod volatility very well. For instance, a white candle means that a stock has increased in price over the course of the day, but the stock may have been experienced strong downward pressure all day until the last few minutes when it suddenly rallied. The candle suggests that the day was bullish, but the true story is a bit more complicated when looking at what really happened.

OTHER CHART TYPES

There are other types of charts that may be useful at certain times. Although day traders do not commonly use them, these charts can provide insights in certain situations, particularly when analyzing opportunities from multiple angles. Many of these charts are exceptionally good at filtering out noise by removing time from the equation and focusing exclusively on price changes and trends occurring over time.

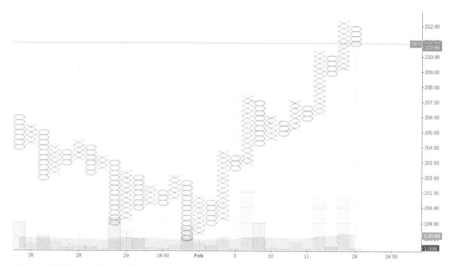

Figure 4. Point & Figure Chart

Figure 4 is an example of a point & figure chart. It may look odd to those who are not familiar with it, but it can prove extremely useful in deciphering key trends.

Some exotic charts types worth knowing are:

- *Point & Figure Charts* These charts consist of columns of X's and O's representing rising and falling prices, respectively. Unlike traditional charts, P&F charts don't plot prices over time but rather price changes, with each new column representing a new trend. The purpose of these charts is to filter the noise and volatility, in order to discern both trends as well as important support and resistance levels.

- *Renko Charts* Renko charts are similar to P&F charts in that they take price change into account rather than time, but instead of X's and O's, they utilize blocks that represent fixed price moves. The benefits of these charts are similar to the benefits of P&F charts, in that they filter out noise to make trends and key price levels easier to recognize than when using traditional charts.

- *Heikin-Ashi Charts* These charts look at two time periods instead of one, and calculate an average in order to smooth out price trends. Since they do not provide specific prices, they aren't all that useful for day traders, except for identifying long-term trends in order to ensure they are trading along-side the prevailing trend.

Traders have a number of choices when it comes to chart types, but the best option depends on the given situation. For instance, a day trader looking at a dense amount of past data for long-term trends may prefer a line chart to remove the noise, while a day trader looking at a one-minute chart may prefer candlestick charts for the added information benefits they provide.

PRICE SCALES

Most charts are created by displaying prices on the Y-axis and time on the X-axis to show the movement of an asset's price over time. While this concept may seem pretty straightforward, there are actually two different ways that prices along the Y-axis are structured that can have a significant impact when analysing a chart. Novice traders should familiarize themselves with these two *price scales* in order to avoid problems during analysis.

The two different price scales are:

- *Linear* When prices along the Y-axis are equally spaced apart, with each space representing an absolute change in the stock price, then the chart is known as linear. The easiest way to know if a chart is linear is to look at the spacing between prices to check if they are approximately equally spaced apart from each other.
- *Logarithmic* When prices along the Y-axis are spaced apart so that each space represents a percentage change in the stock price, then the chart is known as logarithmic. The easiest way to know if a chart is logarithmic is to look for the spacing between higher prices to decrease (since there is less of a percentage change).

The logarithmic price scale is widely preferred in the financial markets, since it better reflects changes in value over time. For example, a stock that has increased 10% per year over the past 20 years will have a chart showing slow growth early on and then rapid growth later on. The reality of the situation is that the growth has remained constant, which is reflected in a logarithmic chart that would show a fairly straight upward sloping line.

QUICK RECAP

- Day traders rely on charts to provide instant insights that support their trading decisions. There are many different types of chart to consider. Bar charts and candlestick charts are the two most commonly used charts in the market.

- Bar charts provide insight into price action that distinguishes between the open, high, low, and close, while enabling day traders to look at a greater number of periods in a single chart than crowded candlestick charts do.

- Candlestick charts provide the greatest amount of information in a single chart, with open, high, low, close, and directional information. The chart is only useful for shorter timeframes, even though there are many different types of candlestick analysis.

- Candlestick patterns—such as bullish engulfings or doji stars—are great tools for determining short-term entry and exit points in the context of longer-term patterns or price movements. Nonetheless, traders should always look for confirmations.

- Day traders should familiarize themselves with the many other types of chart available in order to maximize their competitive edge, including Point & Figure Charts, Renko Charts, Heikin-Ashi Charts, and a number of others.

||||||||||||||||||||||

7

TECHNICAL ANALYSIS

Suppose that you're asked to estimate the population growth for a city over the next five years given the historical trends over time in order to support a public works project. While determining the *exact* number of citizens may be more difficult than winning the lottery, relatively straightforward statistics provide a way to quickly and easily forecast the *likely* population in five years. The estimate may not be perfect, but it is likely to be a lot closer than simple guessing, and it's probably good enough to begin work on a project.

Technical analysis is the use of statistics to predict where asset prices are *likely* to be over the coming minutes, days, months, or years. Just as you projected population growth in a way that's better than guessing, day traders use technical analysis to improve the likelihood of success for their trades by taking bets that are better than 50-50. The idea is that making money more than 50% of the time will yield long-term profits, everything else being equal. When combined with proper money management techniques that lead to bigger wins and smaller losses, these dynamics can help generate a significant edge in the market.

In this section, we'll take a look at technical analysis and see how it's used to improve risk-adjusted returns for traders and investors in the financial markets.

TECHNICAL VS. FUNDAMENTAL ANALYSIS

The debate between technical and fundamental analysis is nearly as old as the stock market itself, and there's really no true answer as to who's right.

Technical analysts argue that a company's fundamentals are irrelevant, since the stock price reflects all available public information. In addition, they believe that prices move through interchanging periods of randomness ("sideways trading") and predictability ("trending prices"). The economics of supply and demand, coupled with the underlying psychology of the market, forms the basis for these dynamics. While these predictions may not come true 100% of the time, the better-than-random odds create an opportunity for technical traders.

Fundamental analysts believe that a market's fundamentals drive prices, with everything in-between being random noise. On the one hand, value investors look for companies that are relatively undervalued compared to their peers or their book value. The idea is that the valuation discount will be closed over time as the market realizes it exists. On the other hand, some fundamental investors believe the markets are efficient, and that randomly picking stocks will produce just as much return as hand-selecting stocks in a portfolio.

Others believe in a combination of technical and fundamental analysis in order to achieve the best results. Under this approach, a trader may use fundamental analysis to identify a stock that is undervalued, and then use technical analysis to determine an ideal time to buy when the market is beginning to uncover the true value of the company. Many day traders fall under this category, in that they believe fundamental information can influence prices, while technical factors provide entry and exit points that enhance the odds of success.

TECHNICAL ANALYSIS BASICS

Charles Dow's *Dow Theory* set the stage for technical analysis nearly 100 years ago in a series of editorials published in financial papers. Among other things, the theory states that an asset's price discounts everything, price movements aren't totally random, and "what" is happening is much more important than "why" it's happening. These core theories paved the way to concepts like trending and the idea that statistics can be used to predict price.

Technical analysis is the forecasting of future price movements based on the analysis of past price movements. Whether looking for the market's mood or using statistical analysis, these techniques provide day traders with an idea of what's to come, but not any certainty as to where prices may be headed. A good comparison is predicting the weather, which is generally accurate using various forms of analysis, but can be very wrong in many cases, too.

There are two primary forms of technical analysis:

- *Chart Patterns* Day traders may look at patterns in past prices to get a pulse on the market's underlying psychology in order to make future predictions. For example, an ascending triangle pattern is an indication that bulls are trying to push through a key resistance level and any breakout from that level may be significant.

- *Technical Indicators/Overlays* Day traders may use statistical analysis to determine the strength of price trends and predict either continuations or reversals. For example, moving averages can be used to determine whether prices are higher or lower than they have been over the past 50 or 200 days.

These techniques can provide valuable insights if used properly, but there are many potential issues to consider. Analyzing chart patterns is a very subjective process that's often considered to be more of an art than a science. Technical indicators and overlays may be less subjective in many ways, although they may also point traders in the wrong direction sometimes, particularly if the market's underlying fundamentals change.

When using technical analysis, it is important to keep the fundamentals of the market in mind in order to to avoid any problems. A sudden fundamental change in an economy or security may lead a stock to rise or fall rapidly. In that case, technical analysis can then be used to determine *how far* the stock will rise or fall before reaching a new support or resistance level.

TRENDS & TREND LINES

Most technical analysis is rooted in market psychology at its core, and the idea of trends and trend lines is no exception.

Groupthink is an interesting phenomenon whereby groups of people tend to stick together even if they are headed in the wrong direction. In the financial markets, many bubbles have been caused by this widespread belief that the masses can't be wrong. The U.S. housing bubble, for instance, was instigated by many "professionals" who claimed that the high prices of houses were justified by the demand for them, even though the demand was proven to be unstable due to a rising number of defaults among borrowers.

Trends in the financial markets are a consequence of this kind of groupthink. Even though the fundamentals of companies don't change very frequently, stocks often trend higher or lower based on the market's perception over time. The increase in a stock's price leads to more buyers interested in catching the trend, which leads to further increases in price and a continuation of the uptrend. While these trends eventually reverse direction, the momentum of the moves depends on the group's perception of what's in store for the future.

For example, suppose that Acme Co. announces a new technology product that has consumers buzzing. After reporting strong first quarter results, the stock price may experience a sudden jump followed by a trend higher over the ensuing months, even when no new information is released. The same company might miss analyst expectations during the second quarter, therefore altering the perception of the stock and sending prices lower.

One of the most important phrases for day traders to remember is, "The trend is your friend." When markets are trading sideways, price action often looks random and is very difficult to predict. Trending prices present the best opportunities to profit, as they are driven by an underlying confidence (or

Figure 5. AAPL Uptrend

lack thereof) in a given market. Reversals in those trends, too, present equally attractive opportunities, as the market's reaction is likely to snowball. This tendency again circles back to the idea of groupthink.

Trend lines are commonly used by technical analysts to determine whether a stock is trending higher or lower, and to provide a clear sign as to when the trend is coming to an end.

Uptrends are created by connecting a series of higher lows and higher highs with a continuous upward sloping trend line, which serves as a *support level* for the market. As seen in Figure 5, Apple Inc. experiences an uptrend for about an hour and a half. The price bounces off the upward sloping trend line support several times before breaking down through the trend line and beginning a potential downtrend. Each time the price reaches support, day traders could determine a buying or selling opportunity.

Downtrends are created by connecting a series of lower highs and lower lows in a downward sloping trend line, which serves as a *resistance line* for the market. In Figure 6, Apple Inc. experiences a downtrend that lasts for an

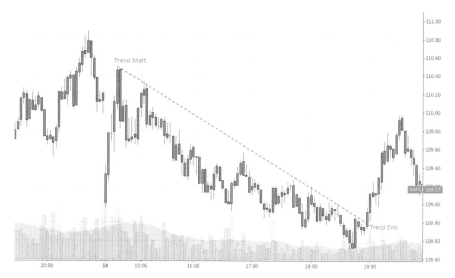

Figure 6. AAPL Downtrend

entire day. The price consistently bounces off of the upper trend line resistance throughout the downtrend. In this case, the trend is still active and won't officially end until the downward sloping trend line is broken through to the upside. Day traders will prefer to enter into short positions during this time, while potentially looking for a breakout of the trend line to confirm a reversal.

When a price is not in an uptrend or downtrend, it is said to be in a state of *congestion* or *consolidation*. Congestion or consolidation occurs when a stock trades either below resistance, above support, or both at the same time. These sideways patterns indicate indecision in the market and make it difficult for technical analysts to predict where prices may be going. Oftentimes, day traders will avoid trading when there's too much indecision in the market, given the inability to predict direction.

The exception to this rule is when stocks are trading in a well-defined price channel, and day traders can buy when the price hits support and sell when it hits resistance. In Figure 7, there are many potentially profitable trading signals generated from these dynamics, even though the stock is not necessarily

DAY TRADING

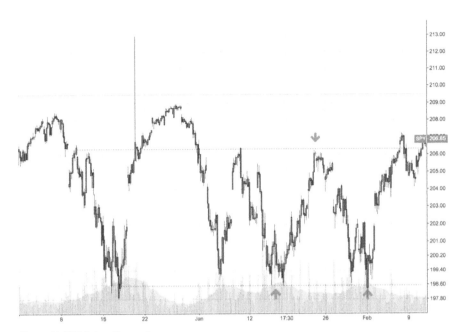

Figure 7. SPY Price Channel

trending higher or lower. The problem is that these signals are not as reliable as those going in the same direction as a prevailing long-term trend, and there's always a risk that the price could break out or break down.

Trends can be short-lived or last a longer time, depending on how long a day trader is watching them. A 52-week one-day chart may show a higher long-term trend, and a one-day, one-minute chart may show a lower short-term trend. Day traders focus primarily on short-term trends as they typically hold stock for only a day. Nonetheless, long-term trends are still important to consider if one wants to get a fuller picture.

For example, a sudden decline that seems random on a one-minute chart could be attributed to a breakdown from a long-term upward trend line on a one-day chart. Day traders should keep an eye on trends occurring throughout multiple timeframes in order to get the complete picture of prices where volatility is likely to be seen.

SUPPORT & RESISTANCE

The concepts of support and resistance form the cornerstone of technical analysis. Whether shown by trend lines or statistics, these key levels represent areas where prices are prone to reversals or breakouts. Support and resistance levels are primarily determined by supply ("bears" or "sellers") and demand ("bulls" or "buyers") dynamics in a given market. Day traders often watch for breakouts, breakdowns, rebounds, or bounces as a sign that one side of the supply versus demand equation is taking control over the other.

Basic Support & Resistance

Support and resistance levels are usually defined as horizontal trend lines that represent prices that haven't been exceeded after repeated attempts. However, the terms are often used interchangeably with any trend line that hasn't been broken after repeated attempts, rather than just horizontal trend lines.

Support levels are prices where demand is strong enough to prevent further price depreciation. As a price moves closer to a support level, buying picks up until it overtakes selling at or near the support level. These support levels can certainly be broken, of course, but history suggests that they remain intact more often than not, until a change in trend takes place. As a general rule, the strength of a support level depends on the number of times that the price has touched it and the volume in the subsequent rebounds from the levels.

Resistance levels are prices where selling or supply pressure is great enough to prevent prices from rising any higher. As the price moves closer to a resistance level, selling pressure picks up until it overtakes buying pressure. Resistance levels can also be broken, but history suggests that they will remain intact. Just like support levels, the strength of a resistance level can be gauged by looking at how many times it has been touched by a price over time.

The key point to remember when it comes to support and resistance levels is that when a support level is broken it turns into a resistance level, and when a resistance level is broken it turns into a support level. At the beginning of each day, day traders should plot these support and resistance levels and

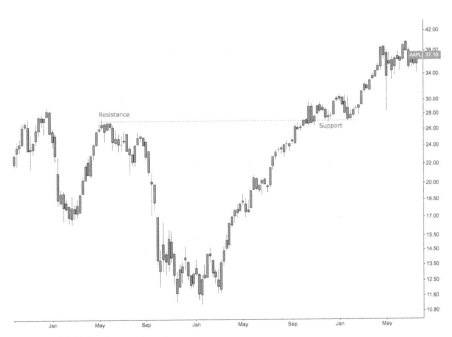

Figure 8. AAPL Resistance Level

remain aware of them throughout the day's trading. These levels are great for
setting potential stop-loss and take-profit points for any trades placed.

In addition to connecting highs and lows, support and resistance levels can
be determined by connecting highs with lows in a horizontal line. Figure 8
demonstrates how a prior resistance level turned into a support level. After
breaking through the 27.00 level, AAPL bulls took over control from the bears
and the prior resistance turned into a support level. Bulls will struggle to
defend the support level, since a break could signal a trend reversal.

Round numbers represent other key areas of support and resistance, since
they are important psychological levels in the market. For instance, many
traders have probably heard financial media pundits discussing whether a
popular index will hold a certain level—such as 10,000 for the Dow Jones
Industrial Average—after a move higher. When prices rise to these levels, selling often intensifies as traders take profit off the table. Prices falling to round
levels see the opposite occur, as traders take the opportunity to pick up shares.

Some day traders identify support and resistance levels at the beginning of the day, and trade based on those levels as their exclusive strategy. For example, a day trader may identify a $10.00 support level and a $15.00 resistance level and focus on entering trades near $10.00 and exiting them near $15.00 using volume as a key indicator of trend strength.

Support and resistance levels aren't restricted to single lines either. In some cases, day traders may identify support and resistance *zones*, which consist of rectangular areas where struggles between bulls and bears intensify. These zones can be identified by looking for concentrations of highs and lows that may be within a price range rather than at a specific set price in general. While zones aren't quite as helpful when setting specific stop-loss and take-profit triggers, they do provide an indication of what to expect.

Finally, day traders should be sure to look at multiple timeframes when identifying support and resistance levels. While traders tend to use short-term charts for their daily trading, it's important to take into account any longer term support and resistance levels in order to avoid placing inopportune stop-loss or take-profit points. An example of where this could become a problem is if a long-term resistance level exists before a short-term resistance level where a take-profit is placed. In this case, the stock might prematurely reverse direction before the take-profit level is hit, and ultimately cause a losing trade as the stop-loss is triggered.

Advanced Techniques

Support and resistance levels may also be calculated using pivot points, chart patterns, or even technical indicators, which adds to the complexity of technical analysis. By combining these various forms of analysis, day traders can identify the most significant areas of support and resistance to watch for a given asset or market. The biggest risk in including other techniques like these is drawing *too many* potential areas of support and resistance on one chart, thus making it impossible to make any decisions.

In Figure 9, day traders can see an example of daily pivot points and the index's movements relative to them. They may not be perfect at predicting areas of support and resistance, but they do provide a good indication of where

Figure 9. Pivot Points

those levels may lie. For example, the first day in February saw the price fall to S1 support, rebound to just above the pivot point, fall lower, and then rebound back above the pivot point to just above R1 resistance.

Popular support and resistance levels include:

- *Pivot Points* Pivot points are simple calculations based on the prior period's open, high, low, and close that are commonly used by all market technicians. Since they are so widely used, prices tend to react to them in a consistent manner.

- *Chart Patterns* Many chart patterns are designed to identify areas of support or resistance that are highlighted using trend lines. In addition to the basic levels, chart pattern provide some insights into *when* breakouts or breakdowns will occur.

- *Technical Indicators* Some technical indicators identify areas of support or resistance (such as Bollinger Bands, where upper and lower trend lines exist), while others simply provide an indication of when prices are too high or too low.

When it comes to generating trading signals, day traders will look toward support levels for buying opportunities and resistance levels for selling opportunities. These dynamics are similar to the "buy low, sell high" saying, an expression popular in financial circles. While some moves below support or above resistance levels may become breakouts or breakdowns, traders should be aware of the potential for *false breakouts* where the moves are merely temporary.

HOW TO CONNECT THE DOTS

Successful day traders must learn to quickly and accurately identify support levels, resistance levels, and chart patterns, especially when using a discretionary trading style. While the concepts seem easy on the surface, drawing trend lines and identifying patterns is as much an art as it is a science. Novice day traders can get a feel for identifying these patterns by analyzing large numbers of charts, making price predictions, and then seeing if those predictions play out in reality, before committing any real capital to trading.

The poker analogy that we used at the beginning of the book holds true here. All poker players should be aware of concepts like pot odds, but the most successful players are those who have picked up cues over time and have learned to "read" other players. In the same way, day traders can understand every statistical component of the market, but the most successful ones are those who get a feel of the market's underlying psychology by "reading" chart patterns.

Many *discretionary* day traders make the majority of their trading decisions based on simple support and resistance levels, combined with an analysis of a stock's order book. For these traders, an understanding of support and resistance levels as well as trend lines may be enough for them to trade successfully over time. *Systematic* day traders, however, rely on a greater understanding of chart patterns and technical indicators when developing trading strategies and systems, from which they would profit over time. These differing levels of understanding suggest that systematic day traders are much more interested in the science behind trading.

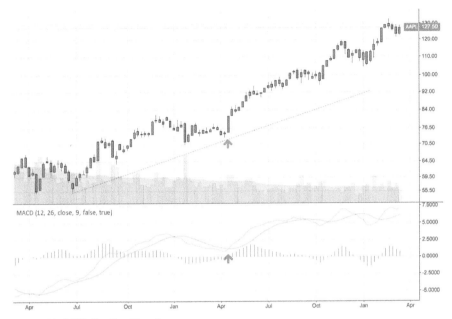

Figure 10. AAPL Trading Signals

After identifying support levels, resistance levels, and chart patterns, the next step is to connect those chart patterns with other forms of technical analysis, such as technical indicators and overlays. Chart patterns provide an indication of *what* will happen in the future; technical indicators help traders *time* successful trades. In Figure 10, a long-term trend line provides a key support level where a day trader may purchase AAPL. The bounce from the support trend line combines with the bullish MACD crossover to provide a strong buy signal that sets the stage for a long-term bullish upswing.

The use of multiple forms of technical analysis at the same time provides *confirmation* that a trade has a high potential for success. In general, the greater the number of signs pointing in a given direction, the greater the odds of a successful trade in that direction. The number of times that a price touches a trend line also provides confirmation of the trend line support or resistance, making it a stronger predictor of a rebound, breakout, or breakdown.

BREAKOUTS & BREAKDOWNS

Day traders like to see sharp price movements. After all, it's much more difficult to make money in the market without any price volatility. Breakouts and breakdowns occur when a price rapidly and significantly moves beyond an expected range. These patterns tend to occur when a price moves sharply outside of the normal support and resistance levels on high volume, although they may also occur at round prices or other significant levels. These breakouts or breakdowns often signify either an acceleration or reversal of an existing trend.

Breakouts occur when a price moves sharply above a key resistance level on high volume. As discussed earlier, the resistance level then becomes a support level to provide a margin of safety as the price trends higher. Day traders often try to buy a security shortly before, during, or just after a breakout, to take advantage of the change in trend. Alternatively, traders may buy the stock after it retraces back to the original breakout point, betting on the fact that the prior resistance has turned into a key support level.

Figure 11. KMPR Breakout Pattern

There are many different ways to identify potential breakouts before they happen. For example, Figure 11 shows an *ascending triangle* pattern in progress. The key level to watch is the upper resistance at around 37.75. If the stock breaks through that level on high volume, the price could jump to the next major resistance at its prior highs of about 41.00. Day traders may also want to keep an eye on other technical indicators, including the MACD, RSI, and momentum indicators, to ensure that the breakout is not a *false* one.

False breakouts happen when the price breaks through a key resistance level and, unable to keep its momentum, moves back below it. False breakouts occur when there is insufficient momentum behind the breakout. Momentum can be measured by looking at volume (e.g., how much is being bought) and price velocity (e.g., how quickly are shares being bought). Since a false breakout represents the inability of bulls to keep momentum, it is considered a very bearish indicator and could lead to a prolonged downward trend.

Breakdowns occur when a price moves sharply below a key support level and the support level becomes a new resistance level. Unlike breakouts, day traders tend to sell or short-sell breakdowns to profit from the rapid drop in price, either when the price breaks below the prior support or after the price rebounds to the new resistance level and moves back down. Short-selling involves borrowing and immediately selling an asset with an agreement to repurchase it at a later date and ideally at a lower price. The practice of short-selling is less popular than buying breakouts, since the risks associated with short-selling stocks are significantly greater than those of long positions. The risks that come with short-selling are less pronounced in markets like options and futures, where long and short risks are equal.

As with breakouts, there are many different ways to identify breakdowns. Figure 12 shows an example of a *descending triangle* followed by a breakdown below key support levels. While the move below 7.60 is a valid breakdown, this chart provides an example of a potentially false breakdown. The downward move occurred on relatively low volume, and the subsequent candle indicates a high level of indecision in the market—two key factors that may force day traders to think twice before placing the trade.

Figure 12. NOK Breakdown Pattern

The key point to remember is that breakouts or breakdowns can quickly invalidate a support or resistance level, which makes them very important to watch. When a breakout or breakdown occurs, the price tends to move rapidly as the opposite side of the market loses confidence in the prevailing trend. A new trend may develop as a result. In such a case, the only thing for which traders must watch out is false breakouts or breakdowns, which can lead to losses.

TRADING GAPS

Sudden price movements are potentially very lucrative for day traders. When prices gap up or gap down, the market may be experiencing a knee-jerk reaction to a very positive or negative event that has occurred, due to the market being thinly traded or closed. These gaps are characterized by two bars (or candles) that are horizontally separated by space between their tails, so a

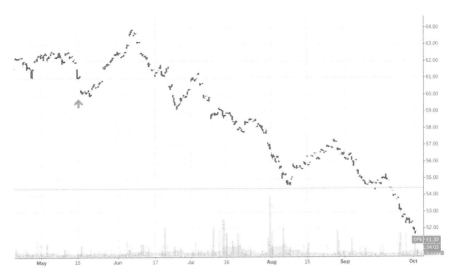

Figure 13. Common Gap

day's high or low doesn't overlap with the other. Day traders can exploit these emotionally-driven reactions to profit.

The majority of gaps occur when the market opens, as overnight or pre-market news is priced into the stock. When stocks are halted or breaking news is announced, gaps may also form as traders are forced to instantly revalue the stock, accounting for the new developments. Gaps can be risky to trade since there is typically very little liquidity during a rapid price movement, which makes it difficult to buy or sell at known prices. Those who trade gaps may not get optimal prices, particularly if they are using market orders instead of limit orders.

Common gaps or *area gaps* are the most basic gaps that occur when a thinly-traded stock goes ex-dividend or experiences a minor hiccup. Most of the time, day traders can ignore these types of gaps, as they are *filled* very quickly. Filling a gap means that after the gap occurs, the price moves to cover the horizontally separated space before moving in a different direction. Day traders may be able to exploit the tendency for gaps to be filled so as to realize small profits, although opportunities are limited.

Figure 14. Breakaway Gap

Breakaway gaps occur when a price experiences a breakout or break-down from a trading range. When this occurs, the breakout or breakdown is instantly validated, and those on the wrong side of the trade tend to quickly head for the exits. These dynamics exacerbate the change in trend and create an opportunity for day traders to jump on the bandwagon. Unlike common gaps, breakaway gaps usually aren't filled very quickly, and instead mark a potential change in the longer-term price trend.

Runaway gaps occur when a price gaps higher or lower in the direction of a trend that already exists. Oftentimes, this occurs when the market suddenly realizes an opportunity and rushes to buy or sell the security all at the same time. Runaway gaps are usually followed by a prolonged move higher in the same direction as the trend, creating an opportunity for day traders to ride the market's coattails for a bit.

Exhaustion gaps occur near the end of a trend and indicate a near-term reversal of the trend. While these can be easily mistaken for runaway gaps, the key difference is that the volume is significantly higher in exhaustion gaps

DAY TRADING

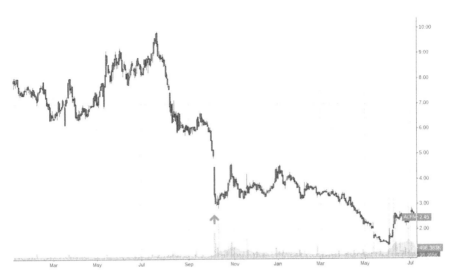

Figure 15. Runaway Gap

due to a struggle between bulls and bears. Exhaustion gaps are also quickly filled as the trend reverses direction, although they often present the best opportunities for day traders to make a profit as they are closed.

CHART PATTERNS

The financial markets are a great example of a complex system—or a system featuring a large number of interacting components whose aggregate activity is nonlinear. In other words, there is no supercomputer in the world powerful enough to decipher what's going to happen next, given the millions of individual traders and investors transacting for millions of different reasons. After all, regulators can't even seem to be able to prevent the most obvious market crashes.

Chart patterns are designed to help day traders make sense of the chaos. Instead of trying to individually analyze millions of transactions, chart patterns visualize data from large groups of transactions. The idea is that certain patterns can be indicative of the market's aggregate mood or psychology at a given point in time. For example, an *ascending triangle* pattern indicates that bulls have been trying to push through a key resistance level for some time and are slowly gaining strength with each attempt, setting the stage for a potential breakout.

There are literally hundreds of different chart patterns developed by technical analysts over the past several decades. In general, there are about 20 chart patterns that are widely used by day traders and should be memorized to assist in their analysis of the markets. It's worth noting that these patterns appear self-explanatory, but using them in practice is more of an art than a science, since prices can be very erratic at times.

Day traders should spend a lot of time studying chart patterns, using them in practice, and learning their finer points in order to become proficient in chart analysis. Most of the time, long-term chart patterns define key support and resistance levels that day traders will watch for rebounds, breakouts, or breakdowns. Short-term chart patterns aren't quite as reliable as long-term chart patterns, but they can still provide some insights worth considering. By looking at multiple timeframes, chart patterns may also overlap so as to provide greater insights.

Head & Shoulders

The *Head & Shoulders* ("H&S") pattern is one of the most iconic chart patterns used to predict a reversal in trend. If properly identified and interpreted, the H&S pattern will provide an accurate prediction of when a trend is coming to an end, as well as specific entry and exit points for trading the reversal. The price targets are not always reached, but H&S price targets provide a useful guideline for day traders wondering how far the reversal will run.

Let's look at an example of an H&S pattern setup:

In the following chart, the low at 61.00 in mid-October marked the end of the first shoulder and the beginning of the head. The same price level was reached in December when the head ended and the second shoulder began. In early 2015, the neckline and trend line was breached and the stock moved sharply lower. The day trader should watch for a rebound to the 62.00 level

Figure 16. BANF Head & Shoulders Pattern

after the move and a high-volume drop that confirms the pattern. When that happens, the long-term change is trend is considered likely to occur.

By measuring the distance between the shoulders and head (or in this case, 8.50), the trader can determine a downside price target (52.50 in this case). This price target provides a rough prediction, but other forms of technical analysis could provide better insights. For instance, a prior long-term trend line or *Fibonacci retracements* (more on this later) may be more accurate, or, ideally, confirm the 52.50 level.

Inverse H&S patterns—as the name suggests—occur when an inverted H&S pattern predicts a bullish change in trend. While many aspects of the inverse H&S are the same as the traditional H&S, the pattern relies more heavily on volume as a confirmation. High volume is nice to have on a traditional H&S pattern when a price breaks down below support, but the inverse H&S *requires* a high volume breakout from resistance in order to be considered valid.

A few other key points include:

- The symmetry of the pattern is important, but not necessary for it to be valid, which means that it doesn't need to be a perfect head and shoulders each time. In general, better symmetry does indicate a more reliable pattern.
- The most critical factor when trading an H&S pattern is properly identifying the neckline support. Once that's done, traders must ensure that the neckline key support is broken on high volume in order to confirm the breakout or breakdown.
- The head should be the deepest part of the H&S pattern, with the shoulders being shallower in nature, although still clearly visible in the pattern. Ideally, the shoulders are equal or roughly equal in height and width.

Triangles

Ascending and *descending triangles* are popular chart patterns for predicting breakouts, which makes them particularly useful for day traders. Oftentimes, the triangles are followed by a breakout in the same direction as the prevailing trend, making them continuation patterns as opposed to reversal patterns. The idea behind triangles is that the market is either accumulating or disposing of shares up until a breaking point or key trend line where the winning side suddenly takes control of the market.

Ascending triangles are bullish chart patterns that occur when a series of higher lows are made with each move higher limited to a horizontal resistance level. As the two trend lines converge, day traders should watch for a breakout to occur on high volume. The price target for an ascending triangle breakout is typically the value of the height of the triangle at the beginning of the formation applied to the upper trend line resistance.

Let's take a look at an ascending triangle pattern:

In Figure 17, BSX begins making a series of higher lows while hitting the same horizontal resistance on the upside. The ascending triangle pattern was followed by a high volume breakout that reached its price target of around 13.85 before retracing. Looking back to late November, the prior high presents another potential trend line resistance that occurs right around the price target predicted by the ascending triangle.

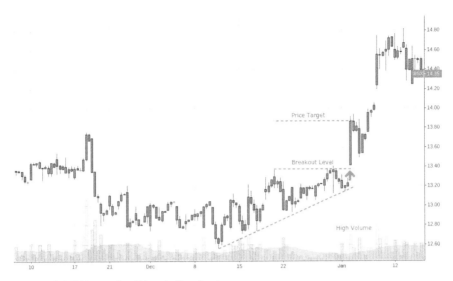

Figure 17. BSX Ascending Triangle Breakout

Descending triangles are bearish chart patterns that occur when a series of lower highs are made with each move lower limited to a horizontal support level. As the two trend lines converge, day traders should watch for a breakdown to occur on high volume. The price target for an ascending triangle breakdown is usually the value of the height of the triangle at the beginning of the formation applied to the lower trend line support level.

Let's take a look at an example of a descending triangle:

In Figure 18, CSLT makes a series of lower highs and even equal lows before experiencing a breakdown on high volume. The stock briefly saw some low volume volatility near its lower trend line before its high volume breakdown over the course of three days, demonstrating the importance of watching for volume as confirmation of a breakdown. In this case, the price target is equal to 4.00 below the lower trend line support or roughly 7.00. A head and shoulders pattern can also be observed over the short term between late November and late December, providing confirmation of a bearish downtrend to come.

Figure 18. CSLT Descending Triangle Breakdown

A few key points to remember include:

- The horizontal resistance or support level in ascending or descending triangles should be tested a minimum of two times, and ideally more than three times. In general, a greater number of reaction lows or highs signals a greater potential breakout.
- Day traders often wait until just after a breakout occurs in order to buy or short, in order to ensure that a valid breakout or breakdown has occurred. For example, a day trader may enter a position ¼ point above the breakout point of an ascending triangle.

Double Tops & Bottoms

Double tops and double bottoms are popular chart patterns that predict a reversal in long-term or intermediate-term trends. After making two attempts at breaking out or breaking down, the chart patterns reflect frustration by the losing side of the bull versus bear battle as they give up the fight. The price targets for these reversals are usually calculated by measuring the

114

distance of the breakout or breakdown point to the peak or trough, and then appending that value to the breakout point in the other direction.

Double tops are bearish chart patterns that occur when there are two peaks followed by a high-volume move lower past key support, which is defined as the low point in the trough between the two peaks. The price target for the chart pattern is defined as the distance from the trough support to the peak, subtracted from the support breakdown. If the peaks are too close or there is insufficient volume associated with the moves, the pattern could simply be prices moving toward a key resistance level rather than a significant trend change.

Let's take a look at a double top chart pattern:

In Figure 19, ROP experiences a double-top pattern that signals an upcoming bearish reversal ahead. The stock briefly rebounds near its prior reaction lows before breaking down sharply below the trend line and confirming the pattern. In this case, the price target would be the difference between the

Figure 19. ROP Double Top Pattern

upper and lower trend lines—or roughly 10.00—applied to the lower trend line—or roughly 140.00.

Double bottoms are bullish chart patterns that occur when there are two troughs that are followed by a high-volume move higher past key resistance. As with double tops, the pattern's price target is equal to the distance between the breakout and the trough lows, and high volume moves off the lows are necessary to confirm the reversal.

Some other important considerations:

- Double tops and double bottoms can't be read in the same way across all chart types. For example, a double top on a line chart is completely different than a double top on a point-and-figure chart or on other charts that discount time.

- Double tops and double bottoms may occur in the context of other chart patterns, such as triangles, which means it's important for traders to look at all the angles.

- Double top and double bottom patterns that occur too closely together tend to be less reliable than patterns that have a greater distance apart.

Rectangles

Rectangles are continuation patterns created by connecting two or more highs and two or more lows with parallel lines that form the top and bottom of a rectangle. Depending on the situation, rectangles may also be known as *trading ranges, price channels,* or *congestion zones.* The pattern is characterized by sideways movement, which represents a pause in the context of a larger trend where bulls and bears are consolidating their positions. The sideways trading eventually culminates in a breakout or breakdown on high volume.

Let's take a look at a rectangle pattern:

In Figure 20, ING forms a rectangle after a significant move higher. The stock trades within the range of several months with three reaction highs and two reaction lows, indicating that the rectangle pattern is valid. After the stock breaks down from lower support on high volume, the pattern is confirmed and a downtrend is likely to ensue. The price target for the pattern is

Figure 20. ING Rectangle Pattern

set by measuring the vertical distance of the rectangle, or roughly 2.00 in this case, and applying it in the direction of the breakdown, or 11.00 in this case.

A few other key points to remember include:

- The breakout or breakdown price should *close* below the pattern in order to confirm the change in direction. When the price fails to close below the upper or lower trend lines, the move may be considered a *false breakout*.
- Rectangles should not be too long or too short in duration—depending on the chart's timeframe—in order to be valid. In general, day traders should watch for two or three reaction highs and lows for a valid rectangle pattern.
- The price often returns to the breakout or breakdown level, which serves as a new area of support in the direction of the new trend. In some cases, the move provides day traders with a second chance to buy into the trade.

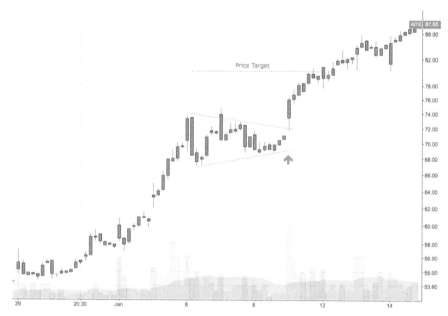

Figure 21. KITE Pennant Continuation Pattern

Flags & Pennants

Flags and pennants are short-term continuation patterns that represent a period of consolidation before returning to the prior trend. After a strong move in either direction, the market undergoes a period of rest during which some traders take profit off the table before the trend resumes in the same direction. The price target for the pattern is calculated by measuring the distance from the base to the breakout or breakdown of the pattern, and applying that distance in the direction of the breakout or breakdown.

In Figure 21, KITE's stock undergoes a sharp run-up in price beginning in early January 2015. The run-up is followed by a period of consolidation that forms a pennant continuation pattern. After the brief period of consolidation, the stock experiences a high volume breakout that reaches the price target almost exactly.

A few important considerations include:

- The sharp move preceding flags and pennants is highly preferred in order for the pattern to be considered valid, although not absolutely necessary. At the very least, flags and pennants with preceding price runs have higher odds of success.
- Look for volume-based confirmation before the pennant or flag, as well as during the consolidation and when the trend resumes. Oftentimes, these confirmations can help day traders avoid false positives and other concerns.

COINCIDENCE OR SYNCHRONICITY

Many fundamental investors dismiss technical analysis as mere coincidence or synchronicity—that is, chart patterns may appear to be meaningfully coordinated but are not causally related to subsequent price changes. Ironically, these same fundamental investors believe that new fundamental developments should be reflected in prices, even though such a correlation is typically only present in the short-term rather than the long-term.

Technical analysts believe that price movements are the result of the market's constantly changing psychological state. For instance, the buyers that emerge at the depth of a recession aren't basing their investments on fundamental developments—since everything is still negative—but rather on the belief that prices themselves are bottoming out. Asset prices during economic crises also tend to be dramatic, with stocks trading far below their fundamental value due to the market's perception of doom and gloom.

While it is impossible to prove whether or not technical analysis *works*, the use of its techniques has become ubiquitous across the financial markets. Technical analysts employ these techniques to decipher the market's psychological state and ultimately arrive at decisions before the crowds. When employed properly, these predictions tend to be accurate more often than not, which suggests that there is some merit to using them.

The tendency of technical predictions to materialize could be due to their predictive abilities or self-fulfilling prophecies. If all day traders are aware of technical analysis and are looking at the same charts, their similar reactions could cause price movements in the direction predicted by the technical analysis. Regardless of the underlying factors at play, there's little doubt that technical analysis serves a key purpose in the financial markets.

QUICK RECAP

- Technical analysis forms the cornerstone of day trading, by providing a framework for predicting future price movements through the statistical analysis of the past. While it is not a silver bullet, technical analysis can improve the odds of success when trading.

- Support and resistance levels are the two most important price areas to consider when day-trading. Oftentimes, these levels are used to determine when to enter or exit a position, and some day traders rely on them exclusively when trading.

- Support levels are prices where a stock tends to rebound higher. The greater the number of rebounds from the same level, the greater the strength of that support level, to which day traders may look to buy a stock ahead of a rebound.

- Resistance levels are prices where a stock tends to bounce lower. As with support levels, a greater number of rebounds lower from the price indicates greater strength for the resistance level, where day traders often look to sell or short a stock.

- Gaps occur when prices move higher or lower without any trading in-between, which forms a visible "gap" on a stock chart. In general, exhaustion gaps get filled while breakaway and continuation gaps do not, presenting a potential opportunity.

- Technical indicators and overlays are used to analyze the statistics associated with past price movements, which makes them ideal for identifying trend strength, gauging price momentum, and determining when a trend is likely to begin or end.

- Chart patterns are used to identify areas where stocks will potentially breakout higher or breakdown lower by looking at areas of support and resistance. In essence, chart patterns are indicative of the underlying market psychology at play.

- Triangle patterns arise when a stock is making consistently higher highs or lower lows with the same support or resistance level capping the moves. Day traders should watch for a breakout from the support or resistance levels as the price band narrows.

- Head & shoulders patterns are reversal patterns that occur when a stock makes a reaction high or low, followed by a new high or low, followed by a lower reaction high or low, representing the inability of bulls or bears to maintain control over price.

- Double tops and bottoms represent a similar psychological state whereby bulls are unable to maintain momentum with double tops, and bears are unable to maintain momentum with double bottoms.

- Flags and pennants are short-term continuation patterns that reflect consolidation—often near a support or resistance level—before a move higher or lower. Day traders may use them as potential opportunities to buy into a trend if they missed it earlier.

||||||||||||||||||||||

8

HOW TO PICK A STOCK

Picking a stock may seem like finding a needle in a haystack, but there are many techniques that can be used to facilitate the search.

Many different factors come into play when picking a stock, depending on the individual's trading style and risk tolerance. Discretionary day traders using Level II quotes and order books as a basis for placing trades usually look at top gainers and losers for the day, to find stocks with the greatest volatility. Systematic day traders employing trading systems may instead look toward technical indicators and chart patterns to identify stocks with *upcoming* volatility in advance of the rapid price movement and volume.

In this section, we'll look at some common techniques used for picking stocks, and some other considerations for day traders.

TOP GAINERS & LOSERS

The most important criterion for many day traders is a stock's volatility. After all, it's impossible to generate a profit from short-term trading without rapid price movement throughout the day.

Top gainers and losers lists provide a great starting point for this type of day trader. By looking at pre-market volatility, traders can identify stocks that are likely to experience big swings during the early morning and late afternoon sessions. The stocks on these lists are usually being driven by fundamental events, such as earnings releases, analyst reports, or other factors, although the movements are subject to technical levels.

These lists can be found in a variety of different sources, ranging from brokerage platforms to financial portals. For example, FinViz.com, a popular financial portal, provides a detailed list of the top movers throughout the trading day. The website also provides insight into what is driving the moves, including new highs, unusual volume, or other indicators.

A common contrarian day trading strategy that's used to capitalize on these movements early on is known as *fading*. When using this strategy, a day trader may wait for a stock to rise to a key resistance level and then short-sell the stock as it moves lower off it. The opposite trade could also be placed, whereby a trader buys a stock reaching new lows as it approaches a key support level. In general, the strategy is aimed at buying into oversold conditions or selling into overbought conditions in order to profit from a regression to the mean.

TECHNICAL INDICATORS & OVERLAYS

Technical indicators are the lines that appear above or below the price on a technical chart, providing some insights into where prices are headed in the future. For example, the Relative Strength Index ("RSI") provides a visual indication of price momentum over time. Technical overlays are a type of technical indicator that appears over the top of price to show various trends

in price over time. For instance, a moving average shows the nth average closing price and applies that value to the current period.

Technical indicators have several different uses:

- *Confirmation* Technical indicators provide confirmation for various
  other forms of technical analysis. For instance, a day trader may identify an ascending triangle pattern and confirm a breakout by looking at a
  MACD crossover.
- *Direction* Technical indicators provide an indication of current and
  future trend direction. For example, a day trader looking to trade in the
  same direction as the prevailing trend may look at moving averages to
  gauge direction.
- *Alerts* Technical indicators alert day traders of potential opportunities and
  hazards. For instance, ebbing momentum could indicate that trends are
  changing and that it might be a good idea for traders to get out of any positions.

Technical indicators provide limited insights when used on their own,
but by using them in conjunction with other forms of technical analysis, day
traders can dramatically improve their odds of success. The key to success
when using these indicators is understanding exactly what they are showing
(e.g. momentum or trend), the most important levels to watch (e.g. 70 and 30
for the RSI) and their limitations (e.g. some of them are only useful in trending markets).

Oscillators

An oscillator is a type of technical indicator that are banded between two
extreme values that are unrelated to price. For instance, moving averages are
a technical indicator overlaid on a chart alongside the price, but moving average convergence divergence ("MACD") is an oscillator with a value that varies
between –100 and +100 regardless of the price. Day traders use oscillators in
order to do things like measure momentum or identify upcoming reversals.

There are two types of oscillators:

- *Centered Oscillators* Centered oscillators fluctuate above and below a
  certain centerline to show strength, weakness, or the direction of price

movement. This type of oscillator often does not have an explicit range limit, but tends to gravitate back toward the centerline over time. MACD is a great example of a centered oscillator that measures the distance between two moving averages—the distance has no limits but tends to gravitate toward the centerline over time.

- *Banded Oscillators* Banded oscillators fluctuate between a defined channel to show when price levels reach extremes. Typically, the oscillator specifies low and high levels that signify oversold and overbought conditions, respectively. The Relative Strength Index ("RSI") is a great example of a banded oscillator where 70 is a universal overbought level and 30 is a universal oversold level.

There are three primary trading strategies that involve oscillators—divergences, crossovers, and breaches. Depending on the oscillators in play, day traders may look at all three of these indicators to determine where prices are headed over the coming ticks.

Divergences are used to predict upcoming reversals in price by looking at instances of oscillators diverging from the underlying prices. When the oscillator is dropping and the price is rising, a negative divergence occurs that could foreshadow a bearish reversal. When the oscillator is rising and the price is dropping, a positive divergence occurs, and a bullish reversal is more likely. The MACD divergence is probably the most heavily watched oscillator for this type of strategy, as it is fairly accurate in predicting reversals.

Crossovers are used to determine a change in the direction of a price trend by looking at centered oscillators. When the price moves below the centerline, a bearish crossover occurs and foreshadows a decrease in the price. When a price moves above the centerline, a bullish crossover happens and an increase in price is more likely to follow. The MACD crossovers are also widely followed in predicting upcoming changes in trends using this strategy.

Breaches are used to predict when prices are getting too low or too high by looking at banded oscillators. When the price moves past an upper band, the consensus is that the security is overbought and due for a correction. When the price moves below a lower band, the market has likely oversold the

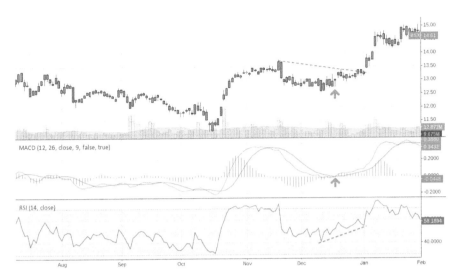

Figure 22. BSX Bullish MACD Crossover

security and it may be due for a rebound. The RSI is the most popular oscillator used for this strategy, where 70 and 30 are the upper and lower bands, respectively.

The best way to implement these strategies in practice is to look at multiple oscillators at the same time and look for these bullish or bearish signals. In addition, day traders should always use oscillators or any other type of technical indicator in conjunction with other forms of technical analysis that can provide a confirmation of their sentiments.

Let's take a look at an example:

In Figure 22, BSX experienced a bullish MACD crossover at a time when the RSI was trending higher. The MACD indicator was also crossing above the zero line, and the RSI remained outside of overbought territory. By reading all of these indicators at the same time, a day trader may have entered into the position at the MACD crossover and exited the position as soon as the RSI reached an overbought level.

Figure 23. SPY Bearish MACD Divergence

Figure 23 shows the concept of divergence, which can be used to predict price reversals, in the case of the S&P 500 SPDR ETF. Between June and August, the MACD was trending lower at the same time that prices were trending higher, which suggested that a reversal was likely to occur at some point. The prediction came true in August, when the price gapped lower and the index fell from nearly 200.00 to nearly 190.00 over a short period of time.

The key to using technical indicators—as with any other form of technical analysis—is to always be on the lookout for confirmations. With many indicators pointing in the same direction, it's much easier for a day trader to justify entering or exiting a trade. Trades with fewer confirmations involve greater risk of a false breakout or breakdown.

VOLUME

Volume is simply the number of shares traded over a given period of time. For example, a stock with a volume of 15 million has transacted 15 million shares throughout the course of the day. If the stock usually trades 10 million shares per day, the increase to 15 million shares may be due to good or bad news during the course of the day. Day traders will typically stick to high volume stocks, since they make it easier to buy and sell at a good price, while also seeking out those experiencing higher-than-average volume as a potential catalyst.

Volume is the single most important source of *confirmations* when using technical analysis, since it provides an idea of the strength behind a price movement. While it's difficult to tell whether a given volume consists of mostly net buyers or net sellers, lack of volume means that breakouts, breakdowns, and other trends could be very short-lived and difficult to predict.

Suppose that a company announces earnings and moves 10% higher in pre-market trading on very little volume. The lack of volume suggests that the 10% may not be all that significant, and the stock could actually move lower when regular trading begins. On the other hand, the same stock experiencing a 10% rise on tremendous volume provides a strong indication that the stock will open and trend higher for the day.

Volume indicators can help interpret volume in the context of price, support, resistance, and other levels in order to improve the odds of success.

There are many different volume indicators:

- *On Balance Volume* On Balance Volume measures buying and selling pressure by adding volume on up days and subtracting volume on down days. Oftentimes, day traders will watch for divergences between these trends and prices in order to determine potential upcoming reversals.
- *Volume by Price* Volume by Price helps visualize the amount of volume for a particular price range, while showing inflows and outflows by color. In general, day traders can use these levels to identify areas of support or resistance.
- *Negative Volume Index* The Negative Volume Index is a cumulative indicator designed to show when the "smart money" is active. In most cases, the odds favor a bull market when the reading is above the 255-day EMA and vice versa.

Day traders can use these volume indicators in a number of different ways.

Figure 24. On Balance Volume

High volume breakouts from trend lines or chart patterns provide *con-firmation* that the pattern's predicted move will occur. For instance, a high volume breakout from a trend line resistance provides confirmation that the breakout is real and the resistance level has become a support level. The lack of confirmation means that day traders should probably avoid a seeming opportunity, due to the high degree of uncertainty.

Volume can also be used as a key indicator of *trend strength*, or whether trends are likely to reverse direction or not. When volume is increasing and prices are losing steam, traders might assume that the trend may be coming to an end over the near-term. The opposite may be true when volume is increasing and price momentum is on the rise, which suggests that the trend remains both intact and very tradable for a day trader.

In Figure 24, On Balance Volume decreased between November and December at the same time that prices were trending higher. The divergence between volume and price action suggested that a correction might occur, which eventually came to fruition in December.

Confirmation

Waiting on the sidelines for a trade to materialize is one of the most difficult parts of day trading, since missed opportunities can be very damaging to the psyche. Traders often eagerly enter into a trade at the first sign of a breakout, breakdown, or other pattern. The problem is that these initial moves can sometimes turn into *false* breakouts or breakdowns, which quickly translate to losses on the trade when prices sharply reverse direction.

Confirmations are technical indicators, chart patterns, volume dynamics or other forms of technical analysis that provide evidence that an initial trading alert is translating into an actual trading opportunity. Day traders should look for at least one and ideally multiple confirmations before committing to a trade, in order to avoid false breakouts and breakdowns. Volume provides one of the strongest confirmations for traders by showing the strength of a move.

For example, a day trader may find a promising breakout ascending triangle breakout pattern that recently moved above the upper resistance level. A novice trader may simply purchase the stock after the breakout to capitalize on the opportunity, but an experienced trader may instead look for additional confirmations first. Without much volume behind the move higher, the experienced trader may not place the trade, and avoid a likely false breakout.

Missing the beginning of a trade (slight profit) or even an entire trade (breakeven) is a better outcome than a *false* breakout or breakdown (loss). By waiting for confirmations, day traders risk missing out on the beginning part of a trade but can still profit from the remaining upside.

Momentum

Volume is a great tool for determining when a trend is gaining or losing momentum, although the dynamics can be somewhat difficult to read. The key to using volume as a momentum indicator is looking at the *direction* of the volume by comparing it with price movements.

On the one hand, accelerating volume would suggest that a trend is picking up steam and is likely to continue on course provided that prices are also accelerating higher. On the other hand, accelerating volume with decelerating prices could suggest the opposite dynamic, where selling pressure is intensifying and bulls are having a harder time pushing prices higher. These same dynamics are true for decelerating volume, which is indicative of a trend that's about to reverse if prices are decelerating at the same time.

MOVING AVERAGES

Moving averages are the most popular type of technical indicator. By averaging prices over time, they enable traders to quickly determine where the current price lies within its historical context. These indicators also help smooth out prices in order to get a clearer picture of long-term and short-term trends, as well as serve as building blocks for more complex technical indicators like the MACD—which essentially measures the distance or gap between short-term and long-term moving averages.

There are three major types of moving averages:

- *Simple Moving Average ("SMA")* Simple moving averages are the most basic type of moving average, calculated by simply taking the mean of n prices, which is designed to show long-term trends in short-term charts.
- *Exponential Moving Average ("EMA")* Exponential moving averages are the most commonly used type of moving average, which calculate the average of all historical price ranges, beginning at the point that the trader specifies.
- *Weighted Moving Average ("WMA")* Weighted moving averages are the third most common type of moving average, which is linearly weighted to ensure that the most recent prices have a greater impact than older prices.

There are advantages and disadvantages associated with each type of moving average. For instance, the weighted moving average is often choppier than the simple moving average, which can make it more difficult to discern market trends. The corollary is that simple moving averages aren't as quick to react to new trends as weighted moving averages, which makes them more of a lagging indicator and potentially less useful in fast-moving markets.

In Figure 25, the blue line represents the WMA, the red line represents the EMA, and the green line represents the SMA. The SMA is the least choppy

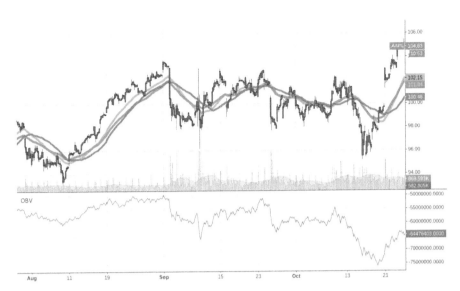

Figure 25. Types of Moving Average

of the three moving averages, while the WMA and EMA tend to move more closely with prices.

Choosing Timeframes

The most important part of using moving averages is determining the appropriate timeframe. When looking for short-term trends, 5- to 20-period moving averages are best suited for determining where prices are headed in the short term. Long-term moving averages consisting of 20 or more periods are ideal for identifying longer-term trends, and can be useful for gaining context when looking at short-term price movements.

The most popular moving average lengths are the 20-day, 50-day, and 5-day moving averages, since they are round numbers that represent psycho-logically important levels. That said, day traders may want to experiment with different lengths when looking at different stocks in order to see what works best for each situation. Traders may also want to use certain moving averages in conjunction with certain technical indicators.

Using Moving Averages

There are many different ways that moving averages can be used to improve trading, ranging from simple trend identification to complex trading strategies.

Moving averages are a great way to identify the *direction* of a trend. By looking at the slope of the moving average, day traders can quickly determine whether prices are generally rising or falling over time. Changes in the slope of the moving average come as long-term price trends are beginning to shift direction, representing potential trend trading opportunities, but, as a general rule, most day traders stick to trading in the same direction as the prevailing trend.

The most commonly used moving average strategy is the *double crossover*, which looks at the dynamics between short-term and long-term moving averages. When a short-term moving average crosses above a long-term moving average, the strategy generates a buy signal due to the short-term trend change relative to the long-term trend. The opposite is true when the short-term moving average crosses below a long-term moving average, which generates a sell signal given the bearish change in short-term trend relative to long-term trend.

In the example above, the slope of the 12-day and 26-day moving averages provides a good indication of when a trend is starting and ending. A day trader may have seen the index's price relative to the average and made sure to stay long-only between mid-October and early December, thus improving the odds of success with everything else being equal. The crossover between these same moving averages also provides a lagging indicator, showing when the trend has begun and ended. It's worth noting, however, that the strategy has limited effectiveness when the price is range-bound.

Finally, moving averages provide great support and resistance levels that day traders should consider when making trades. The most important levels to watch are the round-number psychological levels of 10, 20, 50, and 200, although different stocks may respond best to different moving averages. In many ways, these levels are a bit like a self-fulfilling prophecy, given that they only work because they are so widely watched by traders.

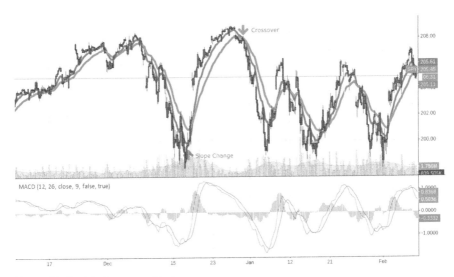

Figure 26. Double Crossover Strategy

Risks & Other Considerations

There are many important risks to consider when using moving averages.

Moving averages are lagging indicators, which means they aren't useful for making snap trading decisions. For instance, a 200-day moving average may be sloping downward long after prices have begun to trend higher. Many day traders use shorter-term moving averages—such as the 10-day moving average—to mitigate some of these concerns, while longer-term moving averages are used to determine trade direction rather than specific executions.

When using the crossover strategy, day traders should also watch out for false signals that can occur in choppy markets. For example, within a sideways market, a short-term moving average may cross above and below a long-term moving average generating a loss each time. Day traders use momentum indicators in conjunction with these types of strategies in order to avoid these situations and accurately identify whether an asset is trending or not.

ELLIOTT WAVES, FIBONACCI & MORE

Technical indicators and moving averages provide day traders with a great starting point for identifying entry and exit points, but there are many other techniques worth exploring as a day trader gains experience over time.

Elliott Waves were developed by Ralph Nelson Elliott to explain the movement of asset prices in response to the underlying market psychology. At its core, the theory suggests that the market moves in predictable patterns consisting of impulse waves and corrective patterns. Traders can decipher these patterns and use them in conjunction with other forms of technical analysis in order to make more informed trading decisions over time.

In Figure 27, Elliott Waves from various timeframes are plotted on the same chart to show the combination of short-term and long-term trends. The Roman numerals represent longer-term waves, while the numbers in parenthesis represent shorter-term waves, although there is some overlap. The full

Figure 27. Elliott Wave Pattern

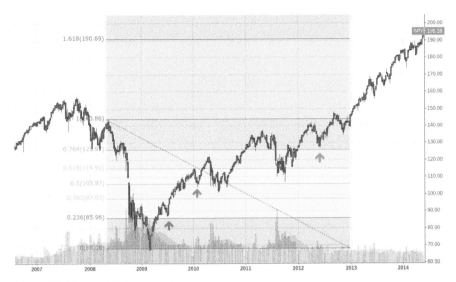

Figure 28. Fibonacci Retracement

spectrum of cycles ranges from Grand Supercycles spanning multiple centuries to Subminuettes spanning just a few minutes.

The Fibonacci sequence is another strategy used to predict areas of support and resistance using mathematics. Developed by the 13th-century mathematician Leonardo Fibonacci, the numerical sequence (and the ratio between its numbers) has been used to describe everything from proportional measurements of the human body to patterns in stock prices. Traders can use these ratios to calculate retracements and a number of other trend lines.

In Figure 28, the Fibonacci Retracement levels from a bearish move in the S&P 500 SPDR ETF provide support and resistance levels to watch. The index rebounded in mid-2009 from the 23.6% level and reacted two more times to the 50% and 61.8% levels. While the Fibonacci tools aren't always 100% accurate, they represent a valuable addition to a day trader's toolbox when it comes to analysing potential opportunities.

These are just two additional techniques that can be used in conjunction with other forms of technical analysis to determine ideal entry and exit points. Over time, traders should experiment with these and other techniques in order to discover what works best for them.

QUICK RECAP

- There are many different ways for day traders to pick stocks, depending on their trading styles and preferences. Discretionary traders often look for volatile stocks in top gainers and losers lists, while systematic traders may look at technical indicators.

- Technical indicators and overlays provide a statistical indication of when stocks are likely to move in certain directions. They can be used in the context of a trading system to screen and identify potential opportunities for entry or exit.

- Volume is one of the most important elements to consider when analyzing potential trading opportunities. It is often used as a confirmation that a trend is beginning or ending, or that a breakout or breakdown is likely to hold.

- Moving averages are a diverse tool that provides day traders with insights as to where the current price lies in relation to its historic norm. In general, the bulls are in control of a market when the price is above the 200-day moving average, and vice versa.

- Elliott Waves, Fibonacci sequences, and other sophisticated techniques exist that traders should also explore in order to find out what works best for them when it comes to identifying entry and exit points in stocks and other financial assets.

9

|||||||||||||||||||||||

TRADING PLAN

Day trading is an incredibly difficult endeavor characterized by low barriers to entry and high competition from experienced and educated professionals. When first getting started, traders should focus on gaining the basic skills necessary to analyze and trade stocks for a living. The most important part of day trading, aside from preparation, is developing a plan that removes emotion from the equation and ensures predictable performance over time. In fact, "plan the trade and trade the plan" is one of the oldest and most widely known phrases in the industry.

As we saw earlier, common cognitive biases and logical fallacies can have a highly detrimental impact on long-term performance. A detailed trading plan can help avoid these emotional landmines by ensuring that decisions are made ahead of time with a cool head rather than in the heat of the moment as an afterthought. For instance, the overconfidence bias can lead to overtrading that leads to costly churn over time. A trading plan reduces overtrading by establishing a system to generate trading signals, rather than relying on instinct.

Trading plans also make it easier to predict trading performance over time. By backtesting and paper-trading strategies, day traders can get a good idea of the returns that they can expect when trading in the market, instead of trying to guess what will happen. A day trader may realize ahead of time that a given strategy has a 20% maximum drawdown, and thus ensure that he has sufficient capital in place to weather the storm, rather than taking on excessive risks that could lead to sharp losses and perhaps even margin calls in times of trouble.

Finally, the trading plan should include detailed record keeping in order to constantly evaluate performance. Many psychological phenomena make it easy to misevaluate past performance, which could lead to day traders losing money without even realizing it. For example, loss aversion could lead to a day trader underperforming the market by refusing to make the right trades over a period of time. By maintaining detailed statistics, these problems can be rapidly identified and avoided, while simultaneously gleaning other important insights.

HOW TO MAKE A PLAN

There are many different elements involved in developing an effective trading plan, depending on a day trader's preferences and trading style. After setting initial goals, traders must build a strategy and consistently monitor their performance to determine if they're on track. Traders who experience lackluster performance might have to revisit their trading plan so that they can either adjust their expectations or their strategies for achieving their desired outcomes.

In this section, we'll take a detailed look at all of these elements and walk you through the steps for creating an effective trading plan.

Getting Started

The first step in developing a trading plan is to obtain a base level of knowledge and experience in the markets. Before embarking on a trading career, aspiring day traders should familiarize themselves with basic concepts such as placing orders, researching stocks, and the ins and outs of various asset classes that they plan on trading. It's also a good idea to begin paper trading in order to get a feel of the day-to-day process until they are comfortable enough using a platform, making quick decisions, and generating their target performance.

After obtaining a base of industry knowledge, day traders should evaluate whether or not they are cut out for the job. The financial risk, emotional stress, and a multitude of other factors involved make day trading a very intense job that's more trouble than it's worth for many people. Traders should be cognizant of these factors and carefully evaluate whether or not they want to pursue this career before going through the work of creating a plan and putting their capital at risk.

Finally, day traders must set the right expectations from the start, based on their financial commitments and paper-trading performance. Without the appropriate expectations in place at an early stage, traders may be setting themselves up for failure.

Building a Strategy

The most difficult part of developing a trading plan is finding a strategy capable of generating a consistent profit over time. While these strategies are constantly evolving, it's important for day traders to document their rules, performance, and changes thereof over time. These records will help ensure that there are records available to evaluate past methods and their successes in different markets to avoid repeating mistakes in the future.

The techniques used to develop these strategies differ depending on the type of trader:

- *Systematic Trading* Day traders who develop specific rules for entering and exiting positions are known as *systematic traders*. Oftentimes, systematic traders will use some form of automation for finding and trading stocks. The use of specific rules also enables them to backtest the strategy against historical data to get an idea of how the strategy will perform over time. For example, foreign exchange ("forex") traders may use *MetaTrader4* software to develop trading systems using the *MQL* programming language that can then be backtested and, eventually, enable them to trade automatically.

- *Discretionary Trading* Day traders who rely on their instincts to enter and exit trades based on real-time data are known as *discretionary traders*. Discretionary traders use tools like intraday charts, Level II order books, and real-time news feeds to identify opportunities and execute trades. Traders using this strategy should paper-trade for an extensive period of time in order to ensure that they are capable of generating consistent performance. For example, a day trader may look at top-movers for the day and buy into a stock with large block bids in the order book, and then sell as the price nears key technical resistance levels and big block asks in the order book.

There is no right or wrong when it comes to choosing between these two trading styles. In general, systematic day traders may benefit from more consistent performance due to their reliance on a well-defined set of rules. Discretionary traders may experience greater variability in their portfolio size over time, but their ability to read the markets might help them adapt more quickly to changing markets and capitalize on unique one-time opportunities.

Managing Money

Money management is the second most important part of a trading plan after the initial strategy development. If risks are not properly managed, day traders may take them on excessively, therefore jeopardizing their entire portfolio without even realizing it. Documenting money management rules can provide a quick reference when immediate decisions need to be made, in order to avoid any potential problems that may arise.

The most important elements of money management to document include:

- *Minimum Bankroll* Day traders must maintain minimum bankrolls in order to comply with rules and regulations relating to financial markets' stability and margin. For pattern day traders, these minimum requirements amount to $25,000 at any given point in time, but all day traders should ensure that they have sufficient capital to trade in the context of their maximum drawdowns and other trading system characteristics.
- *Take-Profit/Stop-Loss* Trading systems should have well-defined take-profit and stop-loss points in order to make the risk/reward profile very clear. Without a stop-loss level in place, day traders could suffer from

cognitive biases that make it difficult for them to sell losing positions and avoid potentially significant downside. Take-profit rules also ensure that traders hold onto winners long enough to enjoy the entire upside.

- *Other Rules* Many day traders implement rules to ensure that they don't let emotion get the best of them. For instance, a maximum daily drawdown may be established in order to avoid the tendency to take on greater risk in an attempt to make back capital that was lost earlier in the day. Such losses can take an emotional toll on anyone, but trading systems can ensure that some of the rules are automatically followed.

The importance of money management cannot be overstated. It is the single greatest barrier against emotional interference in trading. When a position is trading down, traders are tempted to make decisions based on their emotional state, whether that means prematurely exiting the trade or holding on to it far longer than they should, in hopes of a turnaround. Similar dynamics may occur when a position is trading higher and profits are on the table.

Discretionary and systematic traders often employ different types of money management strategies, but both of these types are aimed at achieving the same outcomes. Discretionary traders may manually place stop-loss points and rely on their discretion when calculating take-profit points, while systematic traders may develop an algorithm that automatically sets stop-loss and take-profit points at the moment that a trade is placed.

Keeping Records

Record keeping is an important element of any trading system for two reasons: performance and taxes. Without regular performance reviews, recency bias makes it difficult to objectively know whether a trader is making a profit or loss over time. Performance reviews can also alert day traders when they are beginning to lose an edge due to short-term or long-term changes in market conditions, and help them make necessary changes.

The most important records to keep are:

- *Gain or Loss* The overall gain or loss is arguably the most important metric for day traders to consider, because it accounts for nearly every other factor in play. In the end, more gains than losses are necessary for long-term sustainability.

- *Win/Loss Ratio* The ratio of wins to losses helps day traders determine their success in predicting directional movement. If the average win/loss (see below) is the same, then the win/loss ratio is the sole factor determining profitability.

- *Average Win/Loss* The average win or loss is necessary to determine how much of an edge one is exploiting in the market. If the average win is higher than the average loss, then the trader could get away with an adverse win-loss ratio and still profit.

- *Maximum Drawdown* The maximum drawdown—or the maximum percentage decline experienced during a period of testing—is an important risk factor to consider and helps day traders manage their capital. If the max drawdown is 20%, they should set aside enough capital to avoid a margin call should the worst-case scenario occur.

- *Churn Rate* The number of trades placed in a given period can help a day trader determine if they are overtrading. In general, excessive trading can increase the cost of commissions and make it more difficult to generate a profit.

- *Slippage* Slippage is important for day traders to monitor in order to better predict execution prices for future trades. In illiquid markets, slippage can add significant risks to establishing positions and can affect potential returns over time.

Day traders can track many of these metrics automatically using their brokerage platform, while the data may also be compiled by backtesting an existing trading system against historical data. When just getting started, traders may also want to consider paper trading to see how these metrics compare to backtesting results before committing any real capital. Paper trading simply involves placing fake trades using live data through a brokerage demo account. Traders should watch for even small differences, which can be dangerous when extrapolated over long periods of time and significant numbers of transactions.

Example

A day trader may begin developing a plan of action by identifying a viable trading system. By analyzing different combinations of technical indicators, the trader may find that a moving average crossover strategy combined with MACD convergence/divergence has generated profitable trading signals over the past 10 years. The trader may then decide to try out the strategy by paper-trading in real-time financial markets, making a few changes, and then fully documenting the rules associated with the system.

Next, the day trader will look at the trading system's characteristics to get an idea of how much capital is necessary. The trading system may have a maximum drawdown of 25%, which would require the trader to maintain 25% of capital in cash in order to avoid being wiped out during the worst-case (based on historical prices) scenario. In addition, the trader may decide to stop using the system on any day that experiences more than a 5% drawdown to avoid the tendency to make rash decisions following such losses.

After implementing the trading system with live money, the day trader should keep diligent performance records both for evaluation and tax purposes. These records should consist of detailed transactional data, such as trade symbols, times, and prices, as well as performance metrics, such as profit/loss ratios, average gains/losses, and risk metrics.

QUICK RECAP

- Day traders should have a rock-solid trading plan in place before committing any capital in order to avoid many common pitfalls, ranging from under-capitalization to the inability to determine if they're truly making a profit.

- The first step in developing a trading plan is determining whether discretionary or systematic trading is the best option for an individual. Discretionary traders use their own judgement, while systematic traders rely on established trading systems.

- Day traders should have a sound money management plan in place to limit their risk and ensure the long-term viability of their business. These considerations include things ranging from position sizing to setting automatic stop-loss points.

- Keeping records is a vital activity to ensure long-term success and adaptability to changing market conditions. Day traders should always be looking at statistics like win-loss ratios, average wins, and maximum drawdowns to evaluate their performance.

10

|||||||||||||||||||||||||||||||||||||||||||||

MONEY MANAGEMENT PLAN

Day traders have the potential to make a lot of money, but, oftentimes, the profits associated with trading are highly correlated with the risks taken. In other words, higher returns almost always come at the cost of higher risk.

Money management is the practice of limiting these risks by setting up certain constraints that must be followed. For example, a day trader may set a maximum stop-loss of 5% on any individual trade, which helps limit the risk of any trade to just a 5% loss, with the exception of cases where a lack of liquidity in the market creates slippage or price gaps. These limits can help reduce the risk of a catastrophic loss from a single trade that goes awry, in order to improve risk-adjusted returns over the long-term. In many ways, the practice amounts to answering the question: "How much should you risk on a given trade?"

There are many different possible answers to that question. When it comes to individual trades, position sizing can help determine how much capital to commit to a given position. When it comes to controlling risks associated with a trade already in progress, day traders may want to use stop-loss points or other limits in order to reduce the odds of a one-off catastrophic risk impacting their portfolios. Finally, there are emotional limits that must be placed in order to prevent day traders from losing their nerve.

Money management may also be extended to include the day trader's overall financial situation beyond just trading. For instance, day traders should avoid using any form of loans to finance their business, with the exception of trading on margin. Day traders should also ensure that they have sufficient capital left over to finance their retirement savings and other personal finance accounts, in order to avoid making mistakes that could cost them in the future.

GOALS, BANKROLL, CAPITAL PRESERVATION

The first step in developing an effective money management plan is determining how much capital one should risk in the endeavor.

Day traders should start by calculating how much money they can *afford* to commit to the business. For example, someone with only $30,000 in his bank account may want to think twice before day-trading stocks, since those efforts will require a minimum of $25,000 to get started. It's usually a good idea to avoid taking on outside debt to meet the minimum requirements of day trading given the costs of maintaining these levels of capital, which eat into the bottom line over the long term until the debt is repaid.

The danger with overcommitting is accumulating interest from debt and taking on unnecessary emotional stress. When a trading opportunity arises, the last thing that a day trader needs is a voice in his head reminding him to worry about how to pay next month's rent.

The second major consideration is how much money is *needed* for the effort to be worthwhile. For example, a day trader that requires at least $5,000 a month to live on and only has $25,000 to commit to the business will have a tough time making sufficient returns to sustain his lifestyle. Day traders can help moderate these expectations by starting off in a part-time role—committing to trade only on certain days—or by joining a proprietary trading firm that may be willing to put up some capital for the trader to use.

The third and final consideration is how much money day traders are willing to *risk* at any given time or on a given trade. For instance, a day trader may have $100,000 in starting capital, but may be uncomfortable losing more than 25% of his bankroll. Day traders who are comfortable risking only $25,000 may be forced to implement less risky trading systems with lower average returns in order to have lower maximum drawdown risks. The same dynamics apply when it comes to how much traders are willing to lose *at once* on a given trade.

HOW TO MAKE A PLAN

Day traders should take into account all of the aforementioned factors when developing a money management strategy, in order to avoid many of the pitfalls associated with trading. For example, the amount to risk on each trade is a necessary consideration in order to plan out how many trades can be placed each day and the stop-loss points for those trades.

The first step is establishing how much money one will be committing to day trading, and then using that sum to determine the maximum amount to risk per trade. By setting these limits before placing any trades, day traders can eliminate the temptation to overcommit to a losing trade that could ultimately put the entire account at risk. Margin trading comes into play in making these considerations, since traders are required to maintain a minimum balance in the account in order to avoid margin calls or other potential risks.

The second step is establishing how much risk is acceptable for each trade. Day traders often choose to automatically exit positions where they lose more than a certain amount—such as 5% or 10%—by using stop-loss orders. Setting these maximum expected losses ensures that traders will never be tempted to hold onto losing trades that can prove very costly and dangerous over time. Traders should try to cut losses early, while letting profits run late in order to maximize their overall trading performance.

The third step is to establish a strategy for ensuring the profit goals are being met and for taking money out of the business over time. While most beginners will lose money or break even during the first year or two, the long-term goal is to turn day trading into a business that generates an attractive annual salary. Consistent record keeping should help make it easier to predict how much profit will be generated each month or year. Using that data, day traders can calculate how much they can afford to take out of the market over time.

Day traders should write these three money management rules down on paper, code them into an automated trading system, and/or ensure they are constantly aware of them and following them. Without having a well-defined set of rules, day traders run into costly problems that can quickly eat away at profits over time or quickly implode an account in a short period of time.

The most important part of establishing a money management plan is sticking to the rules consistently over time. Day traders are constantly tempted to break the rules in special circumstances, but—as with trading systems—it's more important to follow the rules than focus on the results. The rules can be changed over time to fine-tune results, since traders will then be fully aware of the consequences, rather than making case-by-case decisions.

QUICK RECAP

- Money management is essential to the success of any day trading operation, since it involves both maximizing profitability and mitigating risk. Ultimately, the key question to ask is how much capital should be risked on each individual trade.

- The amount of profit generated over time is largely dependent on the initial bankroll and the amount of risk a day trader is willing to assume. These metrics must match up with a day trader's expectations in order for them to be successful.

- Capital preservation is just as important as generating a profit, since money lost must be recouped in order for a profit to be made. By locking in profits and establishing strict money management techniques, traders can effectively preserve capital.

- The most difficult step in establishing a trading plan is developing a trading strategy that's capable of generating consistent profit over time. Traders should carefully backtest and paper-trade their strategies to ensure their durability.

- After developing a trading strategy, day traders should carefully document their trading performance for both tax and performance-monitoring reasons. In particular, traders can quickly identify problem areas by regularly reviewing their trading performance.

- Day traders should write down their trading plan and automate as much as possible when it comes to strategy execution and money management. By doing so, they can avoid many of the potential issues precipitated by human emotions.

TRADING

The real fun begins after a day trader has developed a strategy, established a trading plan, and paper-traded for a period of time in order to gain a detailed understanding of the market. While these activities have certainly helped traders prepare, there's nothing like the experience of trading in a live market when real dollars are at risk. Traders should trade conservatively during the first few months, to get a feel of the difference between paper trading and live trading.

In this section, we'll take a look at what happens when traders actually put money into the market, and review some typical daily routines.

BEFORE

A day trader begins the day well before the market opens, with pre-market news, price action, and other factors that could influence prices throughout the day. With a world of information available at one's fingertips, it's important to become proficient at separating what's relevant from what's not. Day traders can eliminate many of these inefficiencies by finding and using the right tools to screen for opportunities and follow up only on what's important.

Some opportunities to watch out for include:

- *Top Movers* Top mover lists highlight stocks that are making strong pre-market higher or lower moves for a variety of reasons. These lists are typically the first stop for day traders looking for opportunities, since they tend to be a strong predictor of future price movement when the market opens.
- *Economic Releases* Macroeconomic releases can have a significant impact on the financial markets, especially for traders focused on trading indexes or currencies. In general, the biggest releases are those covering employment and consumer spending, while some releases impact certain areas of the market more than others.
- *Earnings Releases* Corporate earnings drive stock prices, and earnings releases can cause significant volatility as the information is digested. Oftentimes, stocks will gap higher or lower after a pre-market or after-market earnings release, and then spend the opening hours trying to find an equilibrium price.
- *Analyst Ratings* Analyst upgrades and downgrades can have a significant impact on stock prices, depending on the analyst, company, ratings, and other factors. While analysts aren't exactly known for their long-term accuracy, changes in their ratings are still notable events for traders looking for potential short-term catalysts.
- *M&A Announcements* Mergers and acquisitions are responsible for the majority of volatility in the market, although arbitrageurs quickly close the gaps between purchase and market prices. Day traders often focus on over-reactions to such announcements, or on thinly traded securities that may not immediately move.

In addition to watching for these opportunities, day traders will usually screen for technical opportunities that may arise even with no news at all hitting the wires. Breakouts and breakdowns can occur for a variety of reasons, including things as simple as perceptions or rumors, which may create short-term opportunities to profit. For instance, rumors of a merger in a certain industry may cause speculation across a number of different securities, causing them to break out from their prior resistance and establish new support levels.

The number of positions to have open at any given time depends on many different factors, including the amount of capital available, risk tolerance, and the number of opportunities available to choose from on a given day. Money management techniques often provide a good baseline for the maximum amount of capital to risk on any individual trade, but the true amount depends on the day trader's risk tolerance and confidence about a given trade. The key is ensuring that no individual trade risks a substantial amount of the total capital in a way that could bring the entire portfolio to its knees if the prediction turns out to be wrong.

The next step after identifying opportunities in the market is establishing the plan for when the market opens. Oftentimes, traders will lay out take-profit and stop-loss points for the positions based on technical factors, and will enter those limit orders when the trade is placed in the morning rather than worrying about them after the fact.

DURING

The most important part of a day trader's day is between 9:30 a.m. and 4:00 p.m. eastern time, when the U.S. stock market is open. The greatest volatility is often seen between 9:30 a.m. and 11:00 a.m., with a second wind coming during the latter part of the day, between 2:00 p.m. and 4:00 p.m. Discretionary day traders are often most active in these early and late hours, while systematic day traders don't really focus on any particular time, due to their reliance on a set of rules that could be executed at any time.

Buying

The first opportunity that day traders have to buy is during pre-market, between the hours of 8:00 a.m. and 9:30 a.m. eastern time. During these hours, traders can get a leg up on the competition by acting before the crowd in response to earnings releases and other market-moving events. The tradeoff is that the market is much less liquid, and price discovery isn't quite as certain. For instance, traders may bid up the price of a stock during pre-market hours after an earnings release, but the shares may end the day on a lower note once the numbers are digested. The prices of pre-market trades are often significantly higher or lower than initial market prices. For this reason, traders must establish a new baseline for their assumptions after the open.

The first step in the trading process for most day traders occurs after the market opens. With many different order directions, types, and conditions, day traders should familiarize themselves with the ins and outs of each type of order so that they can make the most suitable choices for themselves. Most traders use limit orders to place long or short trades, and stop-loss orders to limit risk. Stop-limits can be used to set take-profit points, and trailing stop-loss orders can be used to lock-in profits over time as well, creating additional opportunities to fine-tune a trade.

The two possible directions for a trade are:

- *Long* A day trader that buys a stock is said to "be long" in that stock, which was originally intended to mean they were holding it for the long-term. Of course, a trader that's buying a stock is betting on the stock appreciating in price over time.

- *Short* A day trader that bets on a price going down may decide to "go short" on a stock, which involves borrowing shares and selling them with the promise of repurchasing them in the future. Since they receive cash for shares upfront, the idea is that they will be able to repurchase them for a lower price in the future and pocket the difference.

After deciding whether to go long or short on a stock, the next step is to decide what kind of order to place, which dictates *how* the trade is executed. The majority of day traders use limit orders to place trades, since the price is then guaranteed, although only market orders will guarantee that a trader enters a position (regardless of price). The risk with market orders is that the price paid may be significantly higher than the planned amount, particularly during volatile times when prices are moving very quickly in one direction or the other.

Major order types include:

- *Market Order* Market orders instruct a broker to purchase an asset at the next available price in the order book. These orders are designed to execute a trade as quickly as possible without much regard for the execution price.
- *Limit Order* Limit orders instruct a broker to purchase an asset at a certain price or lower in the order book. Unfortunately, these orders cannot be guaranteed, and could lead to some missed opportunities for traders.
- *Stop Loss* Stop loss orders instruct a broker to sell after a stock has reached a certain price in order to prevent further losses. Like market orders, these orders are designed to exit the position as quickly as possible.
- *Stop Limit* Stop limit orders instruct a broker to sell a stock at a specified price and only at that price, which means that these orders have many of the same limitations as limit orders in terms of guaranteed execution.
- *Trailing Stop Loss* Trailing stop loss orders instruct brokers to place a stop order at a defined percentage away from a securities market price, which helps traders protect gains while keeping the position open and exposed to further upside.

After selecting an order type, the next step is to establish how long the order should remain in effect until it's cancelled. Most day traders avoid holding any positions overnight, which means that many of these durations aren't entirely relevant, but provisions like "fill or kill" and "immediate or cancel" shouldn't be overlooked. These provisions can be extremely useful for avoiding partial fills and for precisely targeting near-term opportunities, respectively. In some cases, day traders may use longer durations that last for multiple days.

Major order durations include:

- *Day Order* Day orders instruct a broker to keep an order active until the end of the day and then cancel the order if it isn't filled. Since day traders rarely hold positions overnight, these types of orders are interchangeable with many others.
- *Good 'til Cancelled ("GTC")* Good 'til Cancelled orders instruct brokers to keep an order active until it's cancelled by the trader—even if that means keeping the trade open for several days, weeks, months, or years.

- *Fill or Kill* Fill or kill orders instruct brokers to either execute an entire order or not execute it at all. These order types are useful for avoiding partial fills, which can quickly run up transaction costs and lead to uneven returns for day traders.
- *Immediate or Cancel* Immediate or cancel orders instruct a broker to execute the trade immediately or cancel it entirely. If a day trader is targeting a very near-term opportunity, these orders can be valuable to try to secure a quick execution.
- *On the Open* On the open orders instruct brokers to execute trades as close to the opening price as possible. While they're not always a good idea due to opening volatility, these orders can be useful for buying as soon as possible.
- *On the Close* On the close orders instruct brokers to execute trades as close to the closing price as possible. If the order cannot be executed, the order is canceled entirely and the day trader must hold the stock overnight.

After establishing the order type and duration, day traders must decide if they are going to add any conditions to the order. The most important conditions relate to whether or not an entire order is filled, and how ex-dividends and the like affect limit prices. In general, most traders prefer to use all-or-none orders to ensure that trades are executed at the right price without worrying about partial fills and other similar concerns.

Common conditions for orders include:

- *All or None* All or none conditions instruct brokers to either fill the entire order or not fill the order at all. For example, an all or none limit buy order for 1,000 shares at 15.00 will only be filled if all 1,000 shares can be executed at 15.00 apiece.
- *Do Not Reduce* Do not reduce conditions are restrictions placed on good 'til cancelled orders that instruct brokers to prevent limit prices from being changed due to a dividend when a stock goes ex-dividend.

To summarize, most day traders place fill or kill limit orders designed to ensure that they get a good price and a complete fill. While market orders guarantee execution at *a* price, limit orders ensure that the orders are filled

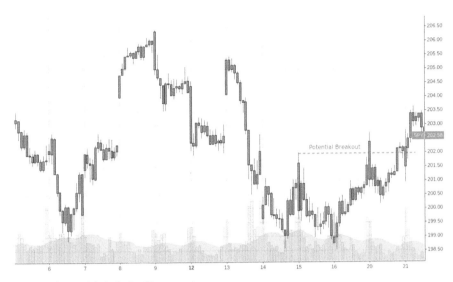

Figure 29. Stop Limit Order Placement

at the *desired* price. The only exception to the rule is when traders are willing to assume the risks associated with slippage in order to guarantee that they receive at least some shares within a specified period of time. For instance, traders may have an exceptionally high-price target after a particular piece of news, whereby they may be able to justify using a market order and paying a higher price to get in on the action.

Day traders set the prices for these limit orders based on either technical or timing factors. For example, a trader may place a stop limit order for a stock that's trading just below a key resistance level within an ascending triangle breakout pattern. The stop limit order's stop price would be placed just above the key resistance level in order to ensure that the breakout occurs before the trade is executed, and a fill or kill order may be used if the price is important. Timing factors may also come into play, such as instances where a trader would like to buy a stock before an earnings release, based on a bet that earnings will beat expectations.

In Figure 29, the SPY closed the previous session nearing its prior highs on strong volume, which suggests that a breakout could occur during the next session. A day trader might consider playing a stop limit order to buy the index at 201.70, which is just above the key breakout level, in order to try and catch a piece of the move near the open. After the trade is established, the trader may place a stop-limit order to sell just below the 201.50 level, which represents a key resistance-turned-support level moving forward.

Systematic traders using trading systems that place trades automatically are free to focus on refining their strategy. In general, these traders will still keep a close eye on trades being executed, in order to ensure that the system is performing correctly—especially when the trading system is new or recently refined. These traders may also have to input certain stocks into a basket to be analyzed, in the event that the trading system doesn't automatically screen for opportunities.

It's also important for all day traders to remain aware of their margin requirements at all times. *Pattern day traders* in particular must maintain $25,000 in equity at any given time in order to avoid account restrictions and potential margin calls. Brokers may have their own requirements geared toward day traders of all types—including minimum margin requirements— that should be understood in detail to avoid costly margin calls or other issues.

Managing Positions

Managing positions requires a combination of careful observation and quick reaction to constantly changing market conditions. While day traders should always have a plan before entering a trade, evolving market conditions mean that these plans could be subject to change over time. Scalpers may be looking to make only a few cents per trade, but longer-term day traders must decide whether to hold on to positions past their preset take-profit and stop-loss points, if the available information suggests there may be a better play in the offing.

For example, a day trader may have shorted a stock that just broke down from support on a high volume with an appropriate price target based on the technical pattern. If a piece of bullish news emerges before the entire position plays out, it's probably a good idea to get out of the positions immediately instead of waiting for the price to hit a preset stop-loss point. A trader could also discover a different market participant placing automated trades and decide to change the strategy in order to take advantage of that insight.

There are three basic possibilities when managing positions:

- *Profit* Day traders should always have take-profit and stop-loss points in mind before entering a trade. As the price approaches the take-profit point, they may decide to let the stock run higher by turning the take-profit point into a new stop-loss point. This leaves room for additional upside for stocks that are continuing to trend higher, while locking in the profits made so far in the trade. After setting this level, some traders will continue to protect profits with a trailing stop-loss order that locks in more profit along the way.

- *Loss* The hardest decisions for day traders to make occur when they sell positions to limit their losses. As the price approaches a stop-loss point, it may be tempting to give the position more room to work, but doing so can be a slippery slope. The key is to avoid rationalization and just take the loss as a cost of doing business as a day trader, and move on to finding new opportunities. If stop-loss points are consistently a problem, traders should reassess their strategies for setting them and look into providing more wiggle room with their trades.

- *Breakeven* The second hardest decision for day traders to make occurs when a position begins to trade sideways without any movement. On the one hand, these situations aren't quite as bad as losses; on the other hand, tying up capital in trades produces opportunity costs. Most day traders will sit on these trades for some time in order to see if a predicted breakout or breakdown occurs, and then simply close the position by the end of the day. If these occur frequently, it may be worthwhile to reexamine the strategy used to select stocks.

Managing positions also requires that day traders weigh opportunities to determine the best places to deploy their capital. For example, a trade that isn't performing as expected may need more time to play out, but a high-potential opportunity that arises could justify selling the stagnant position to take advantage of the new opportunity instead. Traders should carefully consider the costs of such moves as a part of their decision, in order to ensure that the extra churn doesn't adversely affect their portfolio's performance.

Selling

Day traders only consider their top ideas when buying securities, but the notion of only *holding on to* the top ideas is less common. When a trade idea no longer holds its place as a top idea in a portfolio, the trade didn't pan out and it's usually a good idea to sell the stock and move on to different opportunities. Successful traders must be willing to cut their losses and rapidly shift their focus to new opportunities without overtrading, which can result in both missed opportunities (by not waiting long enough) and high costs (through commissions).

Exiting positions can be just as difficult or more difficult than entering them, since there is more of an emotional investment involved. When a position falls in value, many traders find it difficult to exit the trade because it essentially amounts to admitting they're wrong, and there's an element of finality in locking in the losses. Traders must overcome these difficulties and focus on the bigger picture in order to succeed in the long run.

Either a stop-loss trigger or a take-profit trigger should be doing the selling. A stop-loss trigger automatically exits losing positions. A take-profit trigger takes money off the table when a position performs according to expectations. In some cases, day traders will "let their winners run" and won't have a specific take-profit point in mind. The best option in these cases is to slowly reduce their exposure as the stock rises in order to lock in profit over time, while being cognizant of the impact of commissions on these transactions.

AFTER

A day trader's day is not over when the market closes. He must record and evaluate the trades for the day, and then prepare for the next session by catching up on after-market trading action and reading up on any relevant news releases.

Traders should record and evaluate their trades to maintain accurate records and ensure they are not repeating mistakes. Over time, these records can help identify problems with a trading system, which can then be tweaked to improve long-term performance. The records are also useful for reporting purposes, to ensure the accuracy of tax filings.

After recording and evaluating trades, day traders should prepare for the next session by researching after-market trading activity and reading up on the news. After-market trading activity often takes place in stocks that have reported earnings or experienced other market-moving events after the close. These stocks could be potential trading opportunities during the following day's session, or pre-market stocks to watch. Along the same lines, day traders should read up on any market or company news releases that could move the market.

If any interesting opportunities are identified, day traders should write them down and follow-up in the pre-market analysis section of the day.

RISKS

There are many key risks that day traders should keep in mind throughout the entire trading process in order to avoid losses or missed opportunities. From cognitive biases to technical errors, these mistakes are costly but easy to avoid in many cases by simply being aware of them.

The SEC outlines several key risks that day traders should consider before trading in pre- and after-market sessions, since these involve a different set of risks than regular trading hours. While pre-market trading provides traders an opportunity to buy before the crowd, the price isn't guaranteed to carry over to regular hours, and the limited liquidity means that it may be difficult to buy and sell before regular hours begin.

These risk factors include:

- *Quotation Risk* Some firms only allow traders to see quotes from a single trading system that they use in non-market hours trading. Day traders should check with their broker to determine what quotes they see and what quotes are tradable.

- *Limited Liquidity* Pre- and after-market trading has significantly fewer market participants than regular trading hours, which means that there may be less liquidity and it might be more difficult to enter and exit positions.
- *Larger Spreads* The limited number of traders in pre- and after-market hours means that the quoted spreads are often larger, particularly in securities that are experiencing volatility, which can make price discovery somewhat difficult.
- *Increased Volatility* Pre- and after-market trading often has more volatility than regular trading, since there are fewer participants and most traders participating in the market are doing so in order to capitalize on a market-moving event.
- *Uncertain Prices* Pre- and after-market prices do not necessarily reflect the prices at open. In fact, prices often gap higher or lower at the open as the market establishes an appropriate price for the security that involves everyone in the market.
- *Limit Order Bias* Many brokers will only accept limit orders during pre- and after-market trading, which means that the trades may not even be executed if the price isn't reached before the session ends.
- *Professional Competition* Many participants in the pre- and after-market trading sessions are professional traders working for hedge funds or mutual funds, which means that they may have more information at their disposal than retail day traders.

Day traders should also be aware of a number of risks associated with the trading process during regular hours. Some of these risks include certain cognitive biases and psychological tendencies that can prove costly over time. For instance, the confidence bias can quickly lead to a number of trading errors ranging from *averaging down* to *over-margining*.

These risk factors include:

- *Averaging Down* Averaging down involves buying more of a losing position in order to reduce the average purchase price. While the strategy is designed to lower the breakeven point in the event of recovery, it's commonly used as a justification for "doubling down" and can result in steep losses if incorrect.

- *No Diversification* Traders may believe that they have found a winning trade, but without diversification, the risks almost always outweigh the benefits. Of course, most position sizing strategies are designed to mitigate these risks by limiting the amount of capital that can be committed to any individual trade.
- *Irrational Love* Day traders should avoid falling in love with a company's product or management team, and purely focus on the technical of fundamental merits of the trade rather than the long-term viability of the business. In addition, traders shouldn't become emotionally committed to any individual trade, and cut losses when necessary.
- *Illiquid Stocks* Day traders should avoid getting into situations where the securities they're holding could become illiquid—at least without knowing this in advance. These situations may include earnings announcements or halts that could lead to gaps in the stock price where no liquidity is available.
- *Over-Margining* The use of margin is commonplace in the world of day trading, but margin also adds a lot of risk to a position. The use of excessive margin can significantly increase the risk of a trade.

QUICK RECAP

- Day traders have very different workflows depending on their preferred trading style. Discretionary traders are largely focused on capitalizing on short-term opportunities based on support/resistance levels and the order book, while systematic traders are focused on fine-tuning automated trading systems in many cases.

- The beginning of the trading day is often spent screening for ideas and reading about potentially market-moving events set to occur during the day. From there, day traders compile a watch list that will guide the majority of their trading day.

- Most of the volatility in the financial markets occurs during the first couple of hours of trading—between 9:30 a.m. and 11:00 a.m.—and the last hours of trading—between 3:00 p.m. and 4:00 p.m. These hours are important to day traders.

- The three possible scenarios that a day trader faces are: He makes money, he loses money, or he breaks even. Of course, the hardest of these three cases is dealing with losing positions where emotions are running high and as a result traders are prone to committing errors.

- After the market closes, day traders will usually spend some time catching up on any after-hours activity, making notes for the upcoming trading day, and then evaluating their performance in search of areas for improvement.

- Day traders should be cognizant of many risks throughout the day, including their emotions and cognitive biases, as well as those risks associated with pre-market and after-hours trading activities, including the lack of liquidity.

12

‖‖‖‖‖‖‖‖‖‖‖‖‖‖‖‖‖‖‖‖‖‖‖‖‖‖‖‖‖‖‖‖‖‖‖‖‖

TRADING SYSTEMS

Richard Dennis was a commodities trader who became known as *The Prince of the Pit*. In the early 1970s, he borrowed $1,600 and reportedly turned it into $200 million over the course of ten years. Mr. Dennis believed that successful trading could be taught, and recruited 23 aspiring traders to settle the point with friend and fellow trader William Eckhardt. After training the group with a simple trend-following trading system for two weeks, he gave those that showed the greatest promise $250,000 to $2 million of his own capital to trade. The so-called *Turtle Traders* netted a reported $175 million over the next five years following this simple trading system, which clearly defined rules for successful performance.

Nevertheless, it is equally important to note that no trading system performs consistently forever without being modified to fit the changing market conditions. Mr. Dennis learned this lesson throughout the 1980s, when he reportedly lost $50 million between 1987 and 1988 due to the market crash, and again in the late-1990s and 2000s when other market crashes occurred.

In this section, we'll take a look at trading systems, how they are developed, and how they can be used to remove emotion from the trading process and therefore improve performance.

WHAT THEY ARE

Day trading is considered an art by some, a science by some, and a combination of the two by others. In each case, traders develop strategies to capitalize on price action; they then test, practice, and refine these strategies over years until they become consistently profitable. Those who focus on a scientific approach to day trading often rely on *trading systems* to maximize their adherence to the rules and minimize the emotions that are commonplace in the market. Those who choose to place discretionary trades rely on their instincts to do so.

Trading systems are, simply, rules or parameters used to determine when to buy or sell a security over time. These buying and selling *signals* are often plotted on a chart in real time to identify potential trades. *Automated trading systems* will even execute trades on a trader's behalf without him having to lift a finger. These systems help reduce emotional influences in the day trading process. Although the same set of rules won't work forever or in every market, traders who prefer following a system are focused on process over profit.

Most trading systems are based on the interaction between technical indicators, including moving averages and momentum oscillators. By combining two or more of these indicators, day traders can establish a set of rules to determine when a security should be bought or sold. A moving average crossover may produce a *buy signal*, for example, but only if a momentum oscillator is sloping higher and above a zero line to be valid. These rules can be programmed into a software application to automatically generate signals based on real-time pricing data received from stock exchanges or financial data providers.

Advanced trading systems may leverage on other elements that go beyond simple technical indicators. Using pattern-recognition algorithms, some trading systems automatically identify chart patterns that can be incorporated into an analysis. Others read and interpret order books to determine how unexecuted orders may affect prices in the future. And in some cases, neural networks and other advanced mathematical models may be used, in order to identify patterns that may seem entirely invisible to the human eye. Traders using these systems are always pushing the envelope in order to gain the slightest edge in the market.

Many trading systems—especially automated trading systems—include money management rules in order to make position-sizing an objective process. For instance, a trader might specify that only 5% of total capital be risked on any single trade with a trailing stop-loss point that helps limit risks and lock in profit as the trade plays out. Many trading systems use fixed position sizes, percentage of account value, or specific money management systems like the Kelly Criterion or the Larry Williams formulas to optimize position sizing. When implemented properly, these systems can help reduce the risk of catastrophe by limiting the risk exposure for any individual trade in the context of a larger portfolio.

The success of a trading system depends entirely on its rules, which means that day traders spend a lot of time optimizing trading systems to manage risk and improve various performance metrics. Oftentimes, these changes involve modifying specific parameters used within a rule, such as the number of days used to calculate a moving average. A small change in such parameters could produce significant long-term gains, which means that developing and back-testing strategies can pay off significantly over the long run.

Advantages vs. Disadvantages

There are many advantages but also disadvantages to using trading systems, which are important to consider before developing and/or using them. When making the decision, day traders should consider the time they have to devote to honing a trading system, their level of technical expertise, the starting capital they have to invest in trading, and many other relevant factors.

Advantages of trading systems include:

- *Emotionless* By automating the trading process, trading systems remove cognitive biases and other emotional factors that can prove detrimental to trading performance. In the case of automated trading systems, these factors are removed entirely, and the trader must instead focus on improving his trading system's rules over time.

- *Time-Saving* Trading systems help traders focus on refining their technique rather than searching for opportunities every day. In many ways, it's like an executive focusing on how to improve a business rather than spending all of his time filling out paperwork merely to "stay in business."
- *Outsourceable* The development of a trading system can be outsourced to third-party teams. Outsourcing helps speed up the process by eliminating technological procedures. By doing so, a lot of the complexities in programming are avoided, and more time can be spent refining trading rules and optimizing one's performance.

Disadvantages of trading systems include:

- *Complex* Trading systems are often complex in nature. If the process were simple, everyone would be using trading systems to automate becoming rich! The development of an effective trading system relies on a deep understanding of technical analysis, while the constantly evolving nature of the markets means that optimization is always necessary in order to remain profitable over time.
- *Assumptions* Trading systems may appear profitable after backtesting them, but it's important that day traders use the right assumptions in order to ensure their success in real markets. Day traders must account for varying amounts of *slippage* when determining execution prices in backtesting environments, which can be difficult to predict considering the volatile nature of the financial markets.
- *Time-Consuming* Trading systems may save time after they are developed, but creating them in the first place can be very time-consuming. Day traders must have a firm grasp of technical analysis, which can take a lot of time to acquire; even so, finding the right combination of technical indicators to produce consistently profitable trading signals is a profoundly difficult process that is constantly in flux.

Build vs. Buy

Trading systems can either be developed or purchased. There are many advertisements on the Internet for trading systems that promise outlandish returns and that can be purchased for less than $500. While these ads are clearly untrue, since such returns would net the owners billions of dollars over a short period of time, there are some decent trading systems that can be purchased off the shelf instead of starting from scratch. Buying a trading system can help save time and money that would otherwise be spent developing and perfecting such a system.

In general, most day traders are probably better off developing their own trading system instead of buying an existing system off the market. The act of building a trading system itself is a learning process that helps day traders learn about the market and hone their skills over time. For example, experimenting with the interactions between many different technical indicators may help them get a feel for how they work in different markets. Since they are building the system from scratch, they will also inherently understand all of the trading system's components, making it easier for them to modify these components or expand on them in the future.

The "black box" trading systems that can be bought off the shelf are not always transparent about how they work, thus making it difficult to find and diagnose potential problems. For example, a trading system might consistently generate sell signals before a turnaround occurs, leaving room for improvement by modification. Traders who purchase trading systems off the shelf may not know the exact rules the system follows for exiting a position. Without knowing these rules, it is impossible to modify the trading system to improve the timings of sell signals.

Building a Trading System

There are two ways to build a trading system: building it from scratch using a programming language, or building it using an existing software platform in a metalanguage. While there are many differences between these approaches, the idea of establishing a set of rules and parameters to automatically identify and perhaps execute trades remains the same. The choice between the two options depends largely on a day trader's expertise and the complexity of his trading strategy upon implementation.

BUILDING FROM SCRATCH

The most basic way to develop a trading system is to develop it using computer-programming languages, such as *Java* or *Python*. Software developers are very familiar with these languages. Those new to programming, however, will likely have to start from the beginning in order to get a good grasp on the language before they can even begin working on a trading system. The good news is that there are many resources such as books and classes that are designed to help beginner programmers develop the basic skill-sets they would need in order to create these types of systems.

Learning these languages can be a challenge, but they provide the greatest level of flexibility when it comes to designing and implementing trading systems. Many professional traders (e.g., "quants") develop trading systems using these techniques so as to benefit from this level of flexibility and gain an edge in the market.

The process for developing a trading system from scratch includes:

- *Initial Setup* Day traders must set up a simple development environment where trading systems can be developed, compiled, and run. Oftentimes, these setups may consist of a high-performance personal computer and a reliable Internet connection.
- *Data Handling* Price data can be downloaded from free or paid sources, including financial portals, brokerages, or exchanges, and then imported into the application. Live trading environments require reliable and paid data feeds, for obvious reasons.
- *Data Analysis* Third-party packages, like *Panda* for Python, can be used to simplify the process of crunching numbers and avoid having to write low-level code. Using these tools, traders can focus on what's important without worrying so much about the little things.

- *Building & Testing* Day traders must actually build and test the trading system using a combination of data and data analysis libraries. Using historical data, traders can then see how the system would have performed in the past.
- *Integrating* The trading system can be used to generate trading signals that are output to the day trader, or directly sent to a brokerage platform as an actual order using an API, in order to place trades automatically without the day trader's intervention.

There are many different resources on the Internet designed to help anyone learn how to program using languages like Python. With the help of third-party libraries and extensions, day traders rarely have to dive into the difficult part of programming, and are able to focus more on the strategy itself. The only requirement is the time and desire to learn the basics of a programming language and the patience to stick through it.

The biggest risk to consider when developing a trading system from scratch is the introduction of bugs. Since there are no safeguards in place by default, day traders should extensively test the trading system and ensure that there aren't any bugs that may cause incorrect orders or signals, particularly when live-trading. Many libraries include a lot of the core code required to build a trading system, including their own testing suites, but testing full-scale trading systems can be challenging. As a result, traders might also consider outsourcing the development of testing suites to ensure full coverage for their trading systems.

The second-largest risk is the reliability of the data feed and Internet connection, which can result in trades being delayed, executed at the wrong prices, or not even executed at all.

The setup and maintenance of a fully functional trading system build from scratch is beyond the scope of this book, but there are a number of resources available on the Internet and in print for those interested in pursuing these options.

EXISTING APPLICATIONS

The easiest way to develop a trading system is by using existing software. While there is less flexibility built into these solutions, the learning curve is less steep for novice day traders who are just getting started. The ongoing improvements to these applications have made many of them comparable to roll-your-own trading systems that are developed from scratch using programming languages. Some brokers have even rolled out their own platforms with fully integrated metaprogramming languages for developing trading systems.

Here are some of the most popular applications:

- *MetaTrader* (www.metatrader4.com) Day traders focused on the foreign exchange ("forex") markets are probably familiar with MetaTrader, a software platform used by many brokers. MetaTrader comes with a built-in metaprogramming language called MQL.

- *Tradecision* (www.tradecision.com) Tradecision is a higher-end platform designed for active traders. It has a built-in metaprogramming language, extensive backtesting tools, and other unique features, one of which is neural network integrations.

- *TradeStation* (www.tradestation.com) TradeStation is a broker and software platform that's widely popular among day traders. Its metaprogramming language is well known, and code snippets are widely shared on the Internet.

These platforms use *MQL* and *EasyLanguage*, metalanguages that are much easier to learn and understand than programming languages like *C* and *Python*. A trader might need to be familiar with data types and data APIs when building a trading system with traditional programming languages, whereas many metalanguages only require a set of rules programmed using a language very similar to English. Day traders can even buy indicators or trading systems developed by third parties to integrate with their own systems.

Here's an example of a trading rule programmed in TradeStation's *EasyLanguage:*

if HighestBar(AvgTrueRange(14), 14) = 0 then Alert('Indicator is at a high.')

This single line instructs the trading system to alert the day trader if the average true range and the preset trading range are the same, which means that the average true range indicator is at a high. Instead of simply alerting the trader, the same system could instruct the broker to execute a trade or perform any other supported action. The same actions could require tens or hundreds of lines of code using traditional programming languages.

These trading systems are also executed on remote servers, so there is no need to worry about data connections or data feed integrities. The software is maintained by brokers and professionals, so bugs are rare; in the event that any bugs are found, they can be fixed very quickly. The downside is that many of these systems do not have the kind of flexibility that custom-developed applications have.

Buying a Trading System

Day traders who do not want to build their own trading system using programming languages can buy them from third party sources. While buying a trading system is a lot easier than building one from scratch, it is extremely important to test the trading system, understand its risk/reward dynamics, and ensure that returns are generated as advertised before committing any real capital.

In general, trading systems that can be purchased fall under two categories:

- *Trading Software* Trading software is a downloadable or web application that generates trading opportunities based on an underlying algorithm that's applied to a variety of different stocks or assets over a period of time.
- *Trading Signals* Trading signals are opportunities delivered via e-mail, text message, or sent automatically to a broker, and involve less hands-on effort but require a lot more trust in the provider of the trading signals.

These trading systems can be found in a variety of places. TradeStation's TradingApp Store enables developers to sell their trading systems to anyone for a fee, while some other platforms allow third parties to place trades on a trader's behalf.

EVALUATING TRADING SYSTEMS

The most important part of developing or purchasing a trading system is evaluating its performance before committing any capital. While there are entire books written on the subject of performing these types of evaluations, it's important to understand the most common techniques on a high level that day traders can then research in greater detail. The key is generating an environment that's as close as possible to the real thing in order to evaluate how a system performs in that environment over time.

- *Backtesting* Backtesting is the most common technique used to evaluate a trading system. By evaluating the performance of a trading system against a historical dataset, backtesting provides traders with critical pieces of information like net profit, return on capital, commissions paid, total number of trades, win/loss ratio, maximum drawdown, and many other important metrics. Profit distributions may also show how evenly spread the profits and losses were, in order to determine if the system may be relying on pure luck.

- *Monte Carlo* Monte Carlo analysis provides day traders with a great way to test a trading system in a realistic environment. By running the trading system a number of times, each time with a small random change like skipping random trades or changing the order of trades, the Monte Carlo analysis produces statistical performance ranges ("confidence levels") instead of the simple averages seen in most backtesting practices. The maximum drawdowns and other statistical ranges predicted in these simulations can be significantly more reliable than simple backtesting programs that run a single simulation using constant parameters.

Day traders should also be aware of the risks associated with over-optimization or curve fitting when it comes to trading systems. For example, an S&P 500 trading system may have spectacular backtesting results using a simple moving average crossover strategy, making it appear compelling to purchase and implement with live trading. The problem is, the trading system's developer may have used an algorithm that calculated the optimal moving average periods to use given a historical set of data. While these levels may have produced great returns in the past, these past returns are no guarantee that these same levels will produce great returns in the future. The more fine-tuned to the past a trading system is, the more likely that it is ill-suited to predicting future success.

After backtesting a trading system, the next step is paper-trading in the live financial markets in order to gauge its performance. The easiest way to paper-trade is to establish a demo account with a brokerage, and then simply use the trading signals throughout the trading day over the course of a month to see if the results match the backtesting results. While paper-trading doesn't mimic live trading exactly, it's the closest thing to reality and the final step before putting some real capital behind a trading system to see if it works as advertised.

In the end, purchasing trading systems from others involves a high level of trust in the developer or provider. While it's possible to discover flaws through backtesting and other techniques, the ability to generate a consistent profit over time requires hard work on the trader's part in order to ensure that his system remains profitable over the long run. These dynamics are incredibly difficult for professional traders, which means that many trading system providers may provide no more than a limited benefit to those using their systems.

BREAKOUT SYSTEMS

Breakout trading systems are designed to identify prices that are likely to break out from resistance or break down from support. These trading systems are based on programmatically identifying support and resistance levels, and then watching for high-volume breakouts from these points to produce buy signals. These breakouts may be accompanied by supporting factors like favorable momentum oscillator readings or similar technical indicators to provide confirmation and improve the odds of a successful breakout.

The typical trade used to take advantage of a breakout includes a buy order when a confirmed breakout occurs and a stop-loss order simultaneously placed just below the breakout resistance level that has turned into a support level. Of course, the problem is that *false breakouts* can quickly trigger the stop-loss, and losses can pile up. The key to success is developing a solid confirmation strategy to ensure that the breakout is legitimate and more likely than not to continue moving forward rather than whipsawing back down.

Building Blocks

There are many different confirmation strategies to consider, including:

- *Volume* Traders should watch for high volume on any breakout or breakdown, as well as prior volume increases in the same direction of the breakout. Moves toward upper resistance should have higher volumes than moves toward lower support in instances where a trader is about to trade a breakout higher.
- *Momentum* Traders should watch for increasing momentum in the direction of the breakout, which signals that the market is gearing up for the move. Increasing momentum measures the price velocity—or slope of the price movements—which can be a powerful indicator when it comes to breakouts or breakdowns.
- *Timelines* Traders should look at how long it took for the trading channel to develop prior to each breakout or breakdown attempt, as corrections tend to last for comparable periods of time when moves leading into the channels are similar.

Trading systems may either screen for breakout opportunities or look for breakouts in an existing basket of predefined securities. When establishing rules for a breakout trading system, a greater number of rules will generally result in fewer trading opportunities, although they will ideally improve the performance of the trades. These tradeoffs must be carefully considered by day traders in order to determine what is right for them in terms of average win amount and the overall win-loss percentage.

Setting Triggers

Breakout trading systems have well-established buy and sell signals in most cases, since technical patterns provide a great indication of what to expect.

Buy orders can be placed either as the breakout is occurring or after the price moves back to the breakout level. When the breakout is occurring, the buy signal is usually contingent upon the price momentum and volume to confirm that the breakout is legitimate. Day traders who are concerned with a false breakout often wait for a retracement back toward the resistance-level-turned-support-level to occur. A buy order is then placed on the rebound from *that* level to increase the odds of a successful trade.

Stop-loss orders are usually placed just below the breakout level in order to realize the loss before any real damage is done if the move turns out to be a false breakout. In general, the key to placing successful stop-loss orders is choosing a price that does not stop-out trades prematurely, but still limits losses if the trade's thesis turns out to be incorrect.

Take-profit orders are usually placed based on the price target predicted by the technical pattern. For example, a breakout from a channel often has a price target equal to the height of the channel, while a breakout from an ascending triangle has a price target equal to the height of the triangle. Day traders often place take-profit points slightly below these predicted price targets in order to ensure they are executed. Price targets may also be set based on arbitrary gains (e.g., a certain percentage) or based on other technical indicators, like Fibonacci levels, or other longer-term resistance levels.

Example

Suppose that a day trader wants to build a breakout trading system. By looking at the top movers each day, the trader could identify stocks that are likely to experience a new 52-week high, representing a breakout from resistance at their prior high. The trading system might involve entering the trade at the prior high with an automatic stop-loss point just below that level, and a take-profit point that is set at 10% or just below the next resistance level predicted by Fibonacci levels or simple trend lines.

Other Considerations

The efficacy of breakout trading systems is a hotly debated topic, with some experts saying that they're feasible, and others calling them a fool's errand. In general, breakout strategies are more difficult than trend-following strategies, since the day trader is attempting to beat the odds by predicting a reversal rather than going with the odds by following a trend. The tradeoff is that the payout is ideally higher when a reversal is predicted, since the movements tend to be very rapid in nature.

TREND-FOLLOWING SYSTEMS

Trend-following systems are designed to identify trends and create buy signals as a trend is set in motion. As the trade plays out, the trading system looks for signs that the trend is weakening, and issues a sell signal when sideways price movement or a reversal is likely to occur. These trading systems are often based on momentum oscillators and on identifying areas of support or resistance that could create an obstacle for a trend.

Building Blocks

These are the most important indicators to watch for when developing trading systems:

- *Moving Averages* Moving averages provide a great indicator of whether a short-term trend is intact by comparison to a long-term trend. While these are somewhat lagging indicators, they provide insights at a quick glance.
- *Momentum Indicators* Momentum indicators help day traders gauge whether a trend is likely to continue or come to an end, by measuring price velocity. These indicators can help provide timely sell signals to exit a trend.

Setting Triggers

Trend-following systems generally have simple buy and sell signals, as they are largely dictated by the confines of the upper resistance and lower support levels.

Buy orders are placed when prices begin to trend in one direction or the other, and are determined by looking at trend lines, momentum indicators, or other technical indicators. A stock making three consecutive higher lows that can be connected with a straight trend line can be considered in an upward trend; this trend could be confirmed by looking for an RSI reading that is trending higher and above the mid-line.

Stop-loss orders are placed just outside of the trend lines, in order to get out of the position as quickly as possible in the event of an unexpected breakout. Since false breakouts occur regularly, day traders may want to leave some wiggle room for such moves to occur, or build in a way to qualify a sell order with a volume or other confirmation. For instance, a trading system may trigger a stop-loss order if the price moves more than 5% past the upper trend line resistance instead of retreating back toward support levels.

Take-profit orders are typically placed near the opposing trend lines. These orders must often be placed slightly inside of the trend lines in order to avoid missing a rebound, should the price bounce off of resistance or support a bit prematurely. Trading systems may also use technical indicators to predict when trends are losing steam, and generate take-profit orders in that way. For example, a trading system may trigger a take-profit order if the price moves within 3% of an upper resistance level or if the RSI falls below the mid-line.

Example

A trend-following trading system might consist of identifying stocks that have been exhibiting strong upward momentum over the last three trading days. Once the market opens, the system could look for an increase in volume and an ongoing increase in momentum indicators to confirm that the trend is likely to continue and to purchase the stock. The stop-loss point could be set at an arbitrary 5% loss, and then the take-profit point might be set at the nearest resistance level or a simple 5% or 10% gain, with the knowledge that it is more likely than the stop-loss.

Other Considerations

Trend-following systems are probably the most common type of trading system, since many day traders prefer to trade with rather than against prevailing trends. That said, the hardest problems to avoid with trend-following trading systems are false breakouts or breakdowns that can lead to premature buy and sell signals. The other key thing to watch out for is a market that is whipsawing—or sudden increases in price volatility. A whipsawing market can generate many trading signals, each of which incurs a small loss.

CHANNEL SYSTEMS

Channel systems are designed to capitalize on the price movement between support and resistance levels. By taking advantage of the tendency of the price to bounce between these key trend lines, channel-based trading systems can produce buy and sell signals with attractive risk-to-reward characteristics. Traders often incorporate other technical indicators, such as momentum indicators, to improve the risk-to-reward characteristics of such systems and ultimately improve the odds of placing a successful trade.

A simple channel trading system might look for prices moving between two horizontal trend lines with at least four reaction highs and lows. When the price approaches the lower support trend line without any indication of a breakdown, a buy signal is generated and the trader bets on a rebound back toward the upper resistance. The opposite signal is generated when the price approaches the upper resistance trend line without any indication of a breakout.

These systems can be combined with certain elements of break out trading systems to take advantage of situations where the price does breakout or break down. For instance, a day trader may see a breakout, wait for a rebound back to the prior resistance, and then generate a buy signal if a high volume rebound is witnessed. The downside is that these additions introduce an added level of risk, particularly if the trader isn't familiar with breakout trading.

Building Blocks

The most important elements in channel trading systems are:

- *Trend Lines* The upper and lower trend lines provide the entire basis for channel-based trading systems, making them the single most important element for day traders to properly identify.

- *Volume* Volume provides a great indication of whether prices are poised to break out from a channel, since buying interest usually accelerates before a breakout and selling interest usually intensifies before a breakdown.
- *Momentum* Momentum indicators can provide a great confirmation for buying and selling at support and resistance levels. Momentum often decreases as the price approaches these levels, and, if not, traders should watch out for a reversal.

Setting Triggers

The buy and sell signals for channel-based trading systems are relatively straightforward, and are guided by the upper and lower trend line resistance and support levels.

Buy signals are generated when the price is nearing lower trend line support levels, if the appropriate volume accompanies the move. As the price moves toward the support, buying interest should be accelerating in anticipation of a rebound. The opposite is true when the price is moving toward resistance, when selling interest should be intensifying in anticipation of a move lower. Day traders may also want to wait for the turnaround to occur before taking a position, to further avoid the risk of a breakout or breakdown. Combined, these confirmations are necessary in order to avoid breakouts or breakdowns that can prove extremely costly in channel-based trading strategies.

Stop-loss points are typically set just outside of the upper and lower trend line resistance and support levels. Of course, the key is setting these points far enough outside of the trend lines to avoid being affected by false breakouts or simple market volatility. Some channel-based trading systems use volume or technical indicators as a confirmation of a breakout, which then triggers the stop-loss order to be executed.

Take-profit points are typically placed just inside of the opposing support or resistance trend lines. By placing them inside rather than exactly on these trend lines, day traders ensure that they do not miss the order and experience a move against them. Take-profit points may also be set based on shorter-term trends, chart patterns, or technical indicators. For instance, a take-profit signal may be generated if the price is within 5% of the upper resistance trend line and the RSI is below the mid-line, suggesting that the move is losing steam.

Example

A channel trader may identify a basket of securities that are trading within channels and pay close attention to those that are nearing the upper resistance or lower support levels. When the price nears upper resistance, the trader may look to enter a short position provided that an initial reversal is observed and a breakout is deemed unlikely. The opposite may occur when the prices near lower support, where the trader may look to enter a long position provided that the initial reversal is observed and a breakdown appears unlikely to occur.

Other Considerations

Channel-based trading systems are among the most popular systems for day traders, because their rules are very firmly fixed. Day traders have a good idea of when to buy (near support) and when to sell (near resistance) instead of having to guess based on different technical indicators and chart patterns. The downside is that channels are more difficult to identify, and day traders still have to worry about the possibility of a breakout or breakdown.

The two biggest risks involved are:

- *Breakouts or Breakdowns* Breakouts or breakdowns can quickly erase any gains in channel-based trading systems, which means it's important for day traders to confirm that the trend is reversing course before taking a position.
- *Whipsaw* Whipsaw occurs when a market moves erratically between channels without reaching either the upper or lower trend lines. These dynamics cost traders money in the form of opportunity costs. The best way to avoid such dynamics is to look at prior price action for good movement and to watch momentum indicators.

MISCELLANEOUS SYSTEMS

There are many other types of trading systems based on everything from neural networks to order book entries. While beginning day traders should stick to simpler systems to learn the ropes, these alternatives provide advanced traders with new options to explore. It is worth noting, however, that complexity alone doesn't increase the odds of success. Some of the most successful day traders use simple systems to generate long-term profits.

Neural Networks

Neural network–based trading systems use mathematical principles emulating how the human brain works to capitalize on trading opportunities. At a high level, genetic algorithms work by randomly assigning parameters to technical indicators before combining the most successful parameters to form the next generation. The idea is that the most successful combinations will be determined over several generations, taking advantage of technical indicator settings that are indistinguishable to humans.

Of course, neural networks are not holy grails, and are prone to a number of problems that must be carefully considered. The biggest problem relates to "curve fitting," whereby the trading system is over-optimized based on historical data, to the point where it is no longer effective at predicting the future. Traders using these types of trading systems must carefully balance past performance with the generality needed to be successful in the future in order to ensure that the trading system will be effective.

Pattern Trading

Pattern-based trading systems use computer algorithms to identify specific price patterns that statistically perform in a certain way. A pattern-based trading system may identify a bullish engulfing candlestick pattern that is typically followed by a move higher when looking at historical performance data. The trading system may generate a buy signal followed by a sell signal that's dependent on a set move higher.

As with neural network-based trading systems, there are a number of potential problems with pattern trading systems. The most significant issue has to do with risk management, since individual so-called edge cases can erase days' or months' worth of profits. A bullish engulfing could be followed by a gap lower, due to an earnings release that the market had anticipated would beat expectations but actually missed estimates.

Technical Systems

Technical trading systems are based entirely on technical analysis. A trading system may issue a buy signal when the MACD diverges from the stock price for more than a few minutes, suggesting that a reversal is likely to occur. These trading systems are typically grounded in statistics as well, much like pattern-based trading systems, except that they are based on hard numbers rather than pattern-matching algorithms.

As with other trading systems, technical trading systems suffer from unexpected edge cases, which can quickly erase profits. These systems may also be affected by over-optimization and curve fitting, which can make past performance seem great but then hinder the trading system's ability to predict the future. Traders can avoid these pitfalls by establishing the proper risk management protocols and by extensively paper-trading before committing real capital to a trade.

13

RISK MANAGEMENT

Risk management is the single most overlooked factor necessary for being successful at day trading. After all, a trading system may be highly effective at generating a consistent profit over time, but a single trade that goes awry could lead to catastrophic losses. By putting the proper right risk management systems in place, day traders can avoid the emotional roller coaster that typically leads to mistakes, and instead ground their decision making in statistical probabilities to ensure long-term success.

In this section, we'll take a look at some common risk management techniques that can be employed to improve long-term risk-adjusted returns.

EMOTION VS. PROBABILITIES

Humans are terrible at assessing risks without systems in place to take emotion out of the process, which makes day trading risk management exceptionally difficult.

After the terrorist attacks on September 11, 2001, over 1.4 million Americans changed their travel plans in order to avoid flying, even though driving is much more dangerous than flying. Reports on driving fatalities from that year showed that an *additional* 1,000 people died in driving accidents due to their fear of flying. In other words, 1,000 people would still be alive today if they hadn't dramatically overestimated the risk of another terrorist attack on a plane.

The reason that humans tend to mischaracterize risks relates to the way humanity evolved over millions of years. While spiders and snakes generate an innate threat response—even in newborn babies, people don't hesitate to speed in automobiles despite the far greater risk of death, simply because the brain hasn't evolved to generate the correct response. Again, the inability to correctly characterize risk leads to adverse outcomes.

These same dynamics come into play when trading, since human brains aren't designed to estimate these kinds of numerical risks.

Day Trading Considerations

Day traders must constantly divorce their emotion-based beliefs about risk from the actual statistical probabilities in order to gain a clear picture of what's happening and avoid many of the common trading pitfalls. It may be easy to identify and avoid these sentiments at first, but trading is a fast-paced and high-stress environment that inhibits one's ability to think critically, often forcing the brain to rely on emotion to make snap decisions.

Suppose that a day trader has experienced two big wins over the last couple of days. Recency bias may lead the trader to assume that his trading system has been performing exceptionally well, even if its long-term performance has been miserable. With only the latest data in mind, the trader may decide to increase their leverage, with the result that they subsequently amplify their losses as the trading system regresses to the mean. These types of mistakes could be avoided if the trader looked objectively at their long-term performance instead of relying on their emotional gut feeling that only focuses on the most recent performance.

Some common emotional biases are:

- *Confirmation Bias* The tendency for day traders to put more weight on third-party research that supports their own beliefs rather than looking at things objectively. By doing so, traders may be basing their decisions on faulty information.
- *Gambler's Fallacy* The belief that past performance influences the current odds of something happening, such as four down days leading to an up day. Surprisingly, these beliefs are very widespread among traders.
- *Status Quo Bias* The tendency for day traders to stick with what they know rather than branching out with new strategies to capitalize on opportunities. Oftentimes, these tendencies can lead to missed opportunities or greater risk over time.
- *Negativity Bias* The tendency for day traders to place more focus on negative events than positive events, which can lead to unnecessary caution. For instance, many traders will be much more conservative after experiencing a big loss.
- *Overconfidence Bias* The tendency for day traders to overestimate their own abilities relative to the market. If traders are not careful, their overconfidence can lead to problems down the road, such as overtrading or excessive risk-taking.

Risk management *systems* are essential to long-term success because they look objectively at probabilities rather than emotion, and help traders sidestep many of these cognitive and emotional biases. These systems can be developed and implemented in a number of different ways, but at their core, they are designed to remove human decision-making from the trading process, especially at times when humans are prone to making emotionally charged trading decisions.

For example, a day trader's risk management system may automatically calculate position sizes for each trade based on the stock's volatility or other characteristics, in order to prevent overconfidence from generating oversized positions. The same system may also automatically generate take-profit and stop-loss points to remove any emotion from the trades themselves, such as second-guessing one's decision after the trade has already been placed. These risk-management systems can significantly improve long-term performance by eliminating cognitive biases that have a widespread, negative impact on traders.

RISK CONTROL

Day traders can control risk in a number of different ways, ranging from written rules that discretionary traders follow, to rules programmed into trading systems to remove human emotion from the process altogether. Either way, these measures are designed to eliminate decision-making at the moment of a trade when emotions are running high, and instead focus on making decisions during off-hours when cooler heads prevail.

The best ways to control risk when creating a trading system or strategy include:

- *Limited Margin* Day traders should consider limiting the amount of margin that they use in order to avoid the devastating effects of *margin calls.* While some margin is required in order to leverage trades and profit from small price movements, it's important to balance these considerations with the risks associated with borrowing.
- *Extensive Testing* Trading systems and strategies should be extensively tested using both backtesting techniques and paper trading, in order to evaluate risk-reward characteristics to a high degree of certainty. In particular, the average and maximum drawdowns are important characteristics to know and track over time.
- *Solid Requirements* Trading systems should be required to meet certain criteria when backtested and evaluated. For instance, the systems should have a win-loss ratio in excess of 50%, an average win that's higher than the average loss, and a maximum drawdown that's unlike to trigger a margin call or financial distress.

The following are the most common ways to control risk when placing trades:

- *Stop-Loss Orders* Stop-loss orders are designed to limit risk by establishing a maximum (expected) loss for a given trade. Although they are essential for controlling risk, day traders must be careful to place them far enough outside of normal trading ranges to avoid triggering them accidentally and being *stopped out* of a trade.

- *Maximum Daily Loss* Many day traders establish maximum daily limits to their losses in order to prevent emotion from impacting their decision-making. For example, a trader that experiences a steep $500 loss early in the day may not be in the right state of mind to continue trading and try to "make back" the lost money.
- *Daily Profit Targets* Some day traders like to set daily profit targets and stop trading when they reach those targets. In general, these targets force traders to pocket their gains and avoid taking on additional risks throughout the day using "house money."
- *Monthly Audits* Day traders should undergo monthly audits of their financial performance in order to identify areas that they need to improve and ensure that they are not taking on excessive risks when it comes to executing their trading strategies.

These risk control mechanisms may seem obvious—and, in many ways, they are—but the hard part is adhering to them on a regular basis. When it comes to compliance, discretionary day traders should always have a plan *before* they enter a trade. Having a plan means having a defined stop-loss point, take-profit point, and set rules for modifying the trade that can be referenced on a sheet of paper, on the screen, or within an actual outstanding order.

For systematic day traders, compliance is a bit easier, since they can simply program rules into a trading system that makes the decisions for them or places trades on their behalf. The most difficult aspect of the job for these traders is avoiding the temptation to cherry-pick trades or modify trades that are already established, based on their beliefs of the moment. Instead, these traders should let trades play out, and then, if necessary, make changes to the overall trading system in order to fix any errors that they identify.

THE 20 GOLDEN RULES OF DAY TRADING

In this book, we have explored the major areas of day trading, ranging from market mechanics to building an automated trading system. While there are many things to keep in mind, we will end the book with 20 rules that should always be at the top of one's mind when day-trading.

1. *Plan the Trade & Trade the Plan.* The most important part of day trading is having a battle-tested plan and sticking to it. Since trading strategies can be extensively tested, the biggest variable is always the individual day trader's psychology.

2. *Control Risk with Stop-Loss Orders.* Stop-loss orders are an essential component of any day trader's strategy. Without effective stop-loss points in place, a single trade could produce catastrophic losses that may be impossible to recover from.

3. *Always Seek Confirmation.* Trades that are based on a single criterion are rarely successful, and could entail high risks. As a rule, traders should always seek confirmation for their trade ideas from diverse sources.

4. *Look at the Order Book.* The order book provides an invaluable source of information for day traders by showing where actual buy and sell orders are placed at various prices, which can help enormously in daily trading.

5. *Buy Support, Sell Resistance.* The "buy low, sell high" mantra can be more clearly stated as "buy at support levels" and "sell at resistance levels." All traders are looking at the same prices, and these levels are the two most critical to watch.

6. *The Trend Is Your Friend.* Day traders should almost always look to trade in the same direction as the prevailing trend rather than trying to go against the grain. More often than not, trying to "catch a falling knife" will only get you stabbed.

7. *Watch the 200-Day Moving Average.* Traders are generally bullish above the 200-day moving average and bearish below the 200-day moving average, which makes it a key level to watch for anyone trading in the financial markets.

8. *Avoid Trading the Open.* Most day traders are better off avoiding placing trades at the open or during pre-market hours. Since there's not a lot of volume, professionals can easily manipulate these prices to trick retail traders.

9. *Don't Buy Momentum without an Exit.* Day traders should never buy a stock that's moving sharply in one direction or another without a clear exit strategy, such as a key resistance level on the upside and support level on the downside.

10. *Reversals Happen Slowly.* A stock will rarely change direction suddenly and never retest the prior high or low. Oftentimes, traders should wait for a confirmation to take advantage of these opportunities.

11. *Wait for the Right Opportunities.* Overtrading can be very costly for day traders given that commissions and spreads already eat up razor-thin profit margins. By acting like a sniper rather than an infantryman, traders can target only the best opportunities.

12. *Cut Losses Short & Let Profits Run.* Traders have a hard time admitting when they're wrong and cutting losses short, while it's tempting to lock in profits by selling prematurely, but both of these habits can prove costly over the long run.

13. *Learn to Trade Short and Long.* Many day traders don't like short-selling because of the added risks, but avoiding an entire direction in trading can severely limit the number of opportunities available to capitalize on throughout the day.

14. *Be Skeptical of Third-Party Tips & Systems.* It's tempting to take advantage of third-party stock tips or automated trading systems promising high profits, but the vast majority of day traders are better off building their own intuitions and systems.

15. *Don't Look to Trade for Excitement Only.* Most day traders who are looking for a thrill more than a profit will end up losing money over the long run, since they tend to take on excessive risks that endanger their entire portfolio.

16. *Adjust According to Your Finances.* If your personal finances change and the amount traded surpasses your comfort level, withdraw the money needed and don't put off making changes. Excess risk leads to emotion and, oftentimes, to losses.

17. *Get Out of Sideways Markets.* Day traders should avoid tying up too much capital in sideways markets. If a trade doesn't play out as expected, exit the trade and look for other opportunities rather than holding on hoping for a profit.

18. *Look for Divergence Opportunities.* Day traders should look for divergence across many different sources as potential opportunities to profit, ranging from divergences between technical indicators and prices to divergences in correlated markets.

19. *Keep an Eye on Automated Trading.* Blindly following computer-generated trading signals or simply running a program and not monitoring it are

recipes for disaster; traders should always keep an eye on their trading systems to ensure success.

20. *Don't Give Up.* Day trading is an exceptionally difficult industry given the heated competition, constant changes, and ongoing technological improvements. It takes time to develop a consistent and winning trading system.

GLOSSARY

ACTIVE TRADING The buying and selling of securities with the intention to hold them over a short duration of no more than a day.

ALGORITHM A set of rules to be followed in calculations or other operations, which is typically completed by a computer.

ASK The price a seller is willing to accept for a security.

ASSET Property that holds value and is owned by an individual or company.

BACKTESTING The process of applying a trading strategy to historical data to see how accurately the strategy predicted the actual results.

BANKROLL The amount of money that an individual needs to begin trading.

BID The price a buyer is willing to pay for a security.

BLOCK An order for a large quantity of securities, which is often traded at an arranged price between parties.

BOND MARKET A financial market where participants can issue new debt or buy and sell existing debt securities in the form of bonds, notes, bills, etc.

BREAKOUT A price movement through a support or resistance level, which is typically followed by increased volatility on higher volume.

BROKER A person or firm that charges a fee or commission for purchasing or selling securities submitted by a trader or investor.

BUY-AND-HOLD STRATEGY A passive investment strategy where an investor buys stocks and holds them for a long period of time despite fluctuations in the market.

BUYBACK The repurchase of shares by a company to reduce the number of shares in the market.

CARRYING COSTS The price of holding (or carrying) inventory, including maintenance, insurance, and even opportunity costs.

COMMISSION A fee paid by an individual to a broker in order to provide advice and/or purchase or sell a security on their behalf.

COMMODITY A raw material or agricultural product that can be bought or sold, such as gold or wheat.

DEMAND A fundamental economic concept that represents a consumer's desire and willingness to pay a price for a specific good or service.

DERIVATIVE A security that has a price derived from one or more underlying assets.

DIRECT ACCESS BROKER A broker focused on the speed and order execution rather than research and advice.

DIVERSIFICATION A risk management technique utilizing a variety of investments within a portfolio in order to reduce risk and increase returns.

DIVIDEND A distribution of capital paid regularly by a company to its shareholders out of its profits.

EFFICIENT MARKET HYPOTHESIS A theory suggesting that it's impossible to "beat the market" because markets reflect all available information.

EQUITY A stock or other type of security that represents an ownership interest.

EXCHANGE A marketplace where securities are traded in order to ensure fair and orderly trading, as well as efficient dissemination of price information.

EXCHANGE-TRADED FUND ("ETF") A marketable security that tracks an index or basket of assets, which also trades on a stock exchange.

EXECUTION The completion of a buy or sell order for a security.

EXPIRATION The last day that a futures or options contract is valid. After the expiration date, the contract often expires worthless.

FOREIGN EXCHANGE MARKET ("FOREX") A global decentralized market for the trading of currencies, which occurs largely through international banks.

FRONT RUNNING A practice where market makers deal on advance information before their clients have been given the information.

FUTURES An agreement between two parties that's traded on an organized exchange to buy or sell assets at a fixed price to be paid and delivered later.

GLOBAL MARKETS The buying and selling of goods and services between all countries around the world.

HEDGE FUND A limited partnership utilizing high-risk methods, such as short-selling, with the hopes of outperforming the average market return.

HERD MENTALITY The tendency of people to be influenced by peers to adopt certain behaviors or follow certain trends.

INFLATION A general increase in prices and fall in the purchasing value of money.

INITIAL PUBLIC OFFERING ("IPO") The first sale of stock by a company to the public by either issuing debt or equity.

INSTITUTIONAL TRADERS Pension funds, mutual funds, money managers, and other investors, which account for most trading volume in the market.

INTERMEDIARY An entity that acts as the middleman between two parties in a financial transaction.

LIBERALIZATION A relaxation of restrictions in the market by a government or other governing body.

LIQUIDITY The degree to which a security can be bought or sold in the market without affecting that asset's market price.

MARKET MAKER A dealer in securities that buys and sells at specified prices at all times.

MARKET PRICE The price of a security when it's sold in a given market.

MATCHING ENGINE A reliable computer located on stock exchanges that matches buy and sell orders.

MERGERS & ACQUISITIONS The buying and selling of companies by other companies.

MUTUAL FUND A professionally managed investment company funded by shareholders that invests in diversified holdings.

ORDER BOOK A list of buy and sell orders for a specific security organized by price and maintained electronically.

OVER-THE-COUNTER A security that's traded outside of a formal exchange, such as the NYSE, NASDAQ, or AMEX.

PASSIVE INCOME Earnings derived from enterprises that an individual isn't actively involved in, such as rental property, limited partnerships, etc.

POSITION The amount of a security that's owned or borrowed by an individual or institutional trader or investor.

POSITIVE-SUM A situation where one person's gain isn't necessarily equivalent to another person's losses.

PRIMARY MARKET A part of the capital market that handles the issuing of new securities on behalf of companies, governments, etc.

PROP TRADING A firm trading stocks, bonds, or other securities with the firm's own money rather than depositors' money.

QUOTE The price of a stock specified on an exchange, which often includes its bid and ask price, last traded price, and volume traded.

RAKE A scaled fee taken by a casino during a poker game up to a predetermined maximum amount (usually 2.5% to 5% of the hand's total).

RAW MATERIALS The basic material used to create a product.

RETAIL TRADERS Individuals that speculate on the exchange rate between different securities.

REVENUE The amount of income that a company or organization receives during a specific period of time.

RIGHT A security that gives holders the option to purchase new shares issued by a company at a predetermined price.

RISK EXPOSURE A quantified loss potential of an investment or trading decision, which is usually calculated based on its probability of occurring.

SECONDARY MARKET A market where investors purchase securities from other investors, rather than from the issuing companies themselves.

SECURITIES & EXCHANGE COMMISSION ("SEC") A government commission created by Congress to regulate securities and protect investors.

SECURITY A fungible and negotiable financial instrument that represents some type of financial value.

SHORT-SELLING The act of borrowing money to buy and immediate sell a stock with the intention of buying it back again at a lower price.

SLIPPAGE The difference between the expected price of a trade and the actual execution price.

SPREAD The difference between the bid and the ask price of a security.

STATISTICALLY SIGNIFICANT The likelihood that something is caused by something else rather than by merely random chance.

STOCK MARKET A market where shares of publicly held companies are issued and traded, which usually occurs via exchanges or over-the-counter.

SUPPLY A fundamental economic concept that represents the total amount of a specific good or service that's available to consumers.

TIGHT MARKET A market with a narrow bid-ask spread characterized by abundant liquidity and high volume trading.

TREND The general direction of a market or of the price of an asset, which can be short, intermediate, or long term.

UPWARD BIAS The tendency for a price of a security to move higher over time.

VOLUME The number of shares traded in a security or an entire market during a given period of time.

ZERO-SUM A situation where one person's gain is equivalent to another person's losses.

ENDNOTES

1. http://faculty.haas.berkeley.edu/odean/papers%20current%20versions/individual_investor_performance_final.pdf.

2. http://blogs.scientificamerican.com/cocktail-party-physics/2012/08/27/knowing-when-to-fold-em-the-science-of-poker/.

3. http://www.billionairecensus.com/home.php.

4. Fink, Matthew P. (2008). *The Rise of Mutual Funds*, page 63.

5. http://www.icifactbook.org.

6. http://www.sec.gov/marketstructure/research/hft_lit_review_march_2014.pdf.

7. Data since 2009 has been difficult to find because regulators have shifted focus away from the industry as it has begun to suffer.

8. http://www.sec.gov/marketstructure/research/highlight-2013-01.html#.UlWRTmTEo6F.

9. There's still a lot of research in academia regarding ANN applications to finance, although it's less popular than it was in the 2000s. See: https://scholar.google.com/scholar?as_ylo=2015&q=neural+networks+trading&hl=en&as_sdt=0,6.

10. Speaking beyond just required capital (e.g., in the case of pattern day traders), there are still some restrictions on things like margin in some futures markets.

INDEX